WINES
of
NEW ENGLAND

WINES
of
NEW ENGLAND

Whetstone Publishing
BRATTLEBORO, VERMONT

ISBN 0-9621439-2-8

Text design: Roxanne Morissette
Cover design: James Brisson

Editor: Ricia Gordon
Assistant Editor: Anna George

Photo credits: Dan Woodbury, pages 84, 108, 112; Robert F. George, pages 28, 76,
88, 104; John W. Corbett, page 114. Other photos courtesy of the respective
wineries.
Charts: page 19, courtesy New England Wine Gazette; page 25, courtesy Nashoba
Valley Winery.

Published by Whetstone Publishing
28 Birge Street
Brattleboro, VT 05301

Manufactured in the United States of America

*We welcome your comments and suggestions about this book. After you have used
it, if you have ideas about how the content or the format could be made even more
helpful in future editions, please send your comments to the address above.*

Contents

About this book   **vii**

New England wines and wineries:
A brief history
Harvey Finkel   **1**

Climate, soil, and the struggle for survival:
A New England winemaker's distillation
Howard Bursen   **9**

New England fruit wines: A primer
Jack Partridge   **21**

CONNECTICUT   **27**
   Bishop Farms Winery   28
   Chamard Vineyards   30
   Crosswood Vineyards   32
   DiGrazia Vineyards and Winery   34
   Haight Vineyard   36
   Hamlet Hill Winery   38
   Hopkins Vineyard   40
   Nutmeg Vineyard   42
   St. Hilary's Vineyard   44
   Stonington Vineyards   46

MAINE   **63**
   Bartlett Maine Estate Winery   64
   Down East Country Wines   66

MASSACHUSETTS   **73**
   Chicama Vineyards   74
   Inn Wines   76
   Mellea Farm Vineyards   78
   Nantucket Vineyard   80
   Nashoba Valley Winery   82
   Plymouth Colony Winery   84
   Via della Chiesa Vineyard   86
   West County Winery   88

NEW HAMPSHIRE   **103**
   The New Hampshire Winery   104

RHODE ISLAND   **107**
   Diamond Hill Vineyards   108
   Prudence Island Vineyards   110
   Sakonnet Vineyards   112
   Vinland Wine Cellars Winery   114

VERMONT   **123**
   Joseph Cerniglia Winery   124
   North River Winery   126

New England's Wine Grapes   **131**

Wine Vocabulary   **132**

New England Wine Organizations   **134**

About this book

WELCOME TO THE WORLD OF New England wines! Whether you're a wine lover with an adventurous palate, a traveler looking for new backroad attractions, or someone who wants to support New England's agriculture and commerce, this book will help you explore the region's wines and wineries and record your discoveries.

These pages describe 27 wineries and list 213 different wines but by the time you finish reading about them there will probably be more. Wineries change hands, new ones open, and new winemakers are hired. Names of wines may get changed for marketing reasons and a particularly good or bad season for some fruit or grape variety may alter the winery's list. A vineyard that used to sell its grapes to a nearby vintner may decide to produce its own wines. All this is part of the fun and adventure of New England wines (and why it's important to keep notes).

You don't have to visit the wineries to taste the wines, but you may have to do a bit of traveling. Some of the wineries don't have an interstate license so you'll have to buy their wines in the state where they're produced. Some wines, as you'll discover, are only sold at the wineries. Still, New England is a small region and from DiGrazia Vineyards in southwestern Connecticut to Bartlett's Maine Estate Winery is less than a day's drive.

The purpose of a wine diary is not to remember past sensations but to improve future ones. Would you buy that wine again? If so, what kind of meal or event would you serve it at? Would it be better chilled or at room temperature? Would you recommend it to a friend? Keep whatever notes will help you be a better consumer—at the checkout counter, in restaurants, and at home.

In addition to the diary pages, we've left a few blank pages at the back of the book for you to create your own index. You can list the wines you've tasted and what diary page you described them on. You can also keep track of your tastings on the pages that tell about the wineries. Each one has a list of the wines produced and you can put the diary page number next to the wine name. However you choose to use *Wines of New England*, many delightful experiences are sure to be in store.

Happy tasting!

New England wines and wineries: A brief history

by Harvey Finkel

AUTUMN IS NEW ENGLAND'S MOST glorious season, and Thanksgiving our quintessential holiday. Preparations for this great reunion feast are enlivened annually by the never-resolved debate about what wine to serve with the turkey.

It was this pleasant problem and an invitation to judge at the first New England Wine Competition in 1980 that awakened my vinous consciousness to the wines of our region. My solution to the Thanksgiving debate was simple. It was based upon historical and geographical relationships, focusing attention upon the holiday itself, the people participating, and the region in which we live. I chose to use wines of New England.

There is sufficient variety of wine from all six states to provide amiable company for all manner of food. In judging at the competition almost every year since the first, I have witnessed the growing quality and success of the wines, as well as a proliferation of wineries, symptomatic of a turning away from plastic food and concocted drink. Individual artisans are growing and raising flavorful raw materials and handcrafting wine, cheese, and other products, much in the manner of European villagers.

HARVEY FINKEL is a wine columnist for the Boston Globe *and other periodicals, an instructor of wine appreciation courses in the Boston area, and a member of the boards of directors of several wine organizations. When not immersed in wine, Dr. Finkel is a professor of oncology and hematology at the Boston University Medical Center.*

More than two dozen wineries now speckle the New England map, and, in addition to the wineries, there are many commercial vineyards. Every now and then, a grower develops an irresistible yen to make wine instead of selling the grapes, so no doubt we will continue to add to the list of wineries detailed in the body of this book.

What makes a good wine?

Wine is commonly made from grapes, but can also be made from other fruit—apples of various varieties, pears, peaches, assorted berries. A few winemakers produce specialty wines, adding, for example, maple syrup or spices to apple. And antique apple varieties have been reincarnated by oeno-archaeologists like Jack Partridge at Nashoba Valley Winery in Bolton, Massachusetts.

Grapes fall into three groups. Native American grapes like the Concord are hardy and productive. They tolerate our harsh winters and are resistant to most diseases. Their wines, however, suffer grievously from their particular flavor, known in winetasting circles as "foxy." The Eurasian *Vitis vinifera*, familiar to us as Cabernet Sauvignon, Chardonnay, Pinot Noir, and Riesling from Bordeaux, Burgundy, Germany, and California, have trouble attaining ripeness in, or even surviving, the rigors of the New England climate. These vines must be grafted onto native American rootstock to resist the ravages of the plant louse, *Phylloxera vastatrix*. Since vinifera gives us all the world's noble wines, grapegrowers expend much effort and study in the proper selection of vineyard site and grape clone for these vines, often exploiting the tempering effect of the sea in southeastern New England. Growing vinifera is never easy.

A yearning for the best of both grape species has led growers to cross native grapes with the Europeans, resulting in many French-American hybrids. (The French tend to call them American hybrids, Americans like to say French hybrids.) Although nice wines are made from hybrids—Seyval Blanc, Vidal Blanc, Vignoles (Ravat), and Marechal Foch are among the nicest—vinifera justly remains the standard.

Winemaking pioneers

Home-grown wine is not at all new to New England. Wine was made from wild native grapes in the Massachusetts Bay Colony in 1630, the first year of settlement. John Winthrop, governor of the Colony, tried growing grapes on Governor's Island in Boston Harbor. There were plantings in Connecticut and southeastern New Hampshire, and, late in the seventeenth century, by the harassed Huguenots in western Massachusetts and Rhode Island. None of these attempts were successful. It is said that the first vines planted in western New York (about 1818) came from Massachusetts cuttings—these likewise failed to thrive. But the great seal of the state of Connecticut, which depicted healthy vines under the motto, *Sustinet Qui Transtulit* (Who Transplants, Sustains), symbolically predicted success.

By the mid nineteenth century, grapes grown along Boston's Charles River were crushed in presses set up under the city reservoir. California wine was sometimes blended with the local product, a practice occasionally repeated in our day. In 1849, Ephraim Wales Bull, an avid experimental viticulturist and teetotaler, discovered and subsequently popularized the Concord grape in the Massachusetts town of that name. It has flourished as a source of juice, jelly, and, unfortunately, wine.

Competent and commercially viable winemaking in New England began in 1964 when John and Lucille Canepa began planting mostly hybrids around Laconia and Meredith, New Hampshire, on the slopes above Lake Winnipesaukee. Their White Mountain Vineyards produced its first wine in 1969. The Canepas have retired, but the winery, now called New Hampshire Winery and managed by Bill Damour, survives on a smaller scale in Henniker, New Hampshire.

The rebirth of wine growing on Martha's Vineyard came through the efforts of George and Catherine Mathiesen and family in 1971 with the planting of Chicama Vineyards in West Tisbury. Their still-evolving style concentrates on vinifera grapes. The Mathiesens have been a valuable viticultural resource to their colleagues, providing counseling and cuttings. Two cottage concerns got started in 1973. Peter and Mary Kerensky's St. Hilary's Vineyard in North Grosvenor Dale, Connecticut, produces less than 200 cases a year from hand-harvested, native grapes, hybrids, and other fruit. Peter passed away in 1989, but the Kerensky family carries on.

Until 1988, the Bacon family grew and vinified vinifera, often with great success, at Prudence Island Vineyards on that hard-to-reach island in Rhode Island's Narragansett Bay. The vineyard is no longer growing grapes or making wine for commercial purposes, but the Bacons still have a stock of their wines for sale, and welcome visitors.

Next came a phantom. I never saw a bottle from South County Vineyards in Slocum, Rhode Island. Nevertheless, Donald Seibert and H. Winfield Tucker made small batches of Pinot Noir, Chardonnay, and Cabernet Sauvignon at irregular intervals between 1974 and 1980. Perhaps, like Brigadoon, South County will surface again.

Jim and Lolly Mitchell's Sakonnet Vineyards —attractively and strategically set near the sea in Little Compton, Rhode Island—was a significant addition to the ranks in 1974. The Mitchells began with hybrids, and moved, by design, to vinifera. They also did seminal work in vine growing and in establishing southeastern New England as a federally recognized, distinctive viticultural appellation. (The area includes coastal vineyards of Connecticut, Rhode Island, and southeastern Massachusetts.) Sakonnet was purchased in 1987 by Susan and Earl Samson who, along with winemaker Jim Amaral and vineyard manager Joetta Kirk, continued Sakonnet's laudable grape growing and wine production. Amaral recently left for the Northwest, and was replaced by experienced Californian, Tom Cottrell.

Some successes, some failures

Moving away from the sea, we find three alliterative wineries in the hills of Connecticut—Haight Vineyard in Litchfield, Hamlet Hill in Pomfret—both founded in the 1975 bumper vintage—and Hopkins Vineyard, founded in 1979 in New Preston. All three produce wines from both vinifera and hybrid grapes.

Since 1976 Pete and Clair Berntson have struggled valiantly to grow Pinot Noir, which is always a struggle, at Diamond Hill Vineyards in cool Cumberland, Rhode Island. Their aim is to achieve a Burgundy-style wine. They also make pleasing fruit wines.

Stonecrop Vineyards, founded in 1977 in Stonington, Connecticut, showed early promise in hybrids and a little vinifera, but succumbed to extra-vinous misfortunes. The Clarke Vineyard in the same neighborhood, planted in 1979, was succeeded in 1986 by the Smith family's Stonington Vineyards, which is still thriving. (The Clarkes may have been among the first grapegrowers in New England's modern wine age, having planted Chardonnay near New Canaan, Connecticut, in the early sixties.)

David Tower's Commonwealth Winery, built in 1978 in Plymouth, Massachusetts, was a productive force in technology—bringing in modern vinification techniques and equipment—and, initially, in marketing. David helped secure passage of the Farm Winery Act, which permitted direct sales from wineries to wholesalers, shops, and restaurants, and to consumers at the wineries. Commonwealth never grew any grapes, and although its wines were good, the winery was a commercial failure, closing its doors in 1988. Forging the way for fruit wines

The dean of fruit winemaking in New England is Jack Partridge of Nashoba Valley Winery. Jack started making fruit wine in 1979 in a basement in Somerville, Massachusetts. The now-attractive facility, located in Bolton, Massachusetts, is surrounded by orchards of unusual apple varieties. The dry apple, pear, and blueberry wines are bona-fide wines. Sweeter, fruitier wines of cranberry, peach, and other fruit, and a dry sparkling apple wine are all of high quality.

New England catches up

In the eighties we saw a steady accrual of wineries to the cool-climate-winemaking ranks, following in the pioneering paths of Canepa, Mathiesen, Mitchell, Tower, and Partridge. Against the odds of fashion and climate, the continued growth of competence in winemaking in New England has been heartening. Once, a period of hit-or-miss apprenticeship and some pretty awful wines seemed a necessary prelude to respectability. We are now witnessing instant competence. As technology catches up with desire, infant wineries are winning at least their share of awards.

I know you will learn a lot from visiting the wineries of New England, and you'll enjoy tasting New England wines. Your fun will be doubled when you select these wines for your own Thanksgiving feast, or for meals and sipping throughout the year.

New England wineries at a glance

WINERY	STATE	FOUNDED	ACRES	No. WINES	GRAPE/FRUIT	OUTPUT
Bartlett Maine Estate Winery	ME	1983	—	18	fruit	16,000 gallons
Bishop Farms Winery	CT	1987	10	3	fruit	700 gallons
Joseph Cerniglia Winery	VT	1986	45	9	fruit	54,000 gallons
Chamard Vineyards	CT	1983	15	3	grape	15,000 gallons
Chicama Vineyards	MA	1971	18	12	grape	15,000 gallons
Crosswoods Vineyards	CT	1981	35	5	grape	16,700 gallons
Diamond Hill Vineyards	RI	1976	4.5	10	grape & fruit	3,600 gallons
DiGrazia Vineyards & Winery	CT	1984	55	10	grape	7,500 gallons
Down East Country Wines	ME	1984	—	4	fruit	7,800 gallons
Haight Vineyard	CT	1975	35	8	grape	12,000 gallons
Hamlet Hill Winery	CT	1974	28	7	grape	47,600 gallons
Hopkins Vineyard	CT	1979	25	9	grape	16,700 gallons
Inn Wines	MA	1984	4	7	grape & fruit	1,000 gallons
Mellea Farm Vineyards	MA	1988	3	4	grape & fruit	2,400 gallons

WINERY	STATE	FOUNDED	ACRES	No. WINES	GRAPE/FRUIT	OUTPUT
Nantucket Vineyard	MA	1986	7	4	grape	6,000 gallons
Nashoba Valley Winery	MA	1980	55	16	fruit	16,700 gallons
The New Hampshire Winery	NH	1964	—	8	grape & fruit	5,000 gallons
North River Winery	VT	1985	2	9	fruit	12,000 gallons
Nutmeg Vineyard	CT	1982	5	12	grape & fruit	2,000 gallons
Plymouth Colony Winery	MA	1983	12	8	grape & fruit	7,100 gallons
Prudence Island Vineyards	RI	1973	12	2	grape	———————
St. Hilary's Vineyard	CT	1979	8	8	grape & fruit	1,000 gallons
Sakonnet Vineyards	RI	1975	40	11	grape	52,400 gallons
Stonington Vineyards	CT	1986	10	4	grape	10,700 gallons
Via della Chiesa Vineyard	MA	1986	15	2	grape & fruit	6,000 gallons
Vinland Wine Cellars Winery	RI	1988	22	9	grape	24,000 gallons
West County Winery	MA	1984	2	5	fruit	2,000 gallons

Climate, soil, and the struggle for survival: A New England winemaker's distillation

by Howard Bursen

"BUT CAN YOU GROW WINE grapes in New England?" As I sit sipping a glass of 1984 Riesling from Connecticut, this question echoes in my mind. I think back to the vintage of '84, and the 38 tons of grapes we harvested that fall at Hamlet Hill Vineyards in Connecticut. Over the past 15 years or so, New England wines have won more than their share of medals in national and international competitions. Even so, many people react with surprise when they find that the excellent wine in their glass was made in one of the New England states. Despite the industry's best efforts to spread the word, you might say that New England wine is a well-kept secret. Welcome to the inner sanctum!

As more vineyards and wineries spring up, it becomes clear that New England constitutes a wine region in the truest sense: wines made here share certain characteristics; they bear a distinctive regional stamp. How can we account for this quality? Is it the soil, the climate, or the varieties of grapes that grow here? I've thought about this question over the last 10 years while pruning in winter, spreading fertilizer in spring, and while stacking boxes of

HOWARD BURSEN is a vineyard and winery consultant. A former president of the New England Wine Council, Bursen spent seven years as winemaker and vineyard manager at Hamlet Hill Winery in Pomfret, CT. He makes his home with his wife, Sally, and daughter, Malana, in Abington, CT.

ripe grapes on the trailer at harvest time. What follows is a distillation of what I've observed in that time.

New England weather: four seasons with a vengeance

In my opinion, the predominant factor, the one that sets the stage for all the others, is our New England climate. In our region, weather patterns determine which grape varieties can be grown, where they can be planted, and even how large a crop they will bear. I am indebted for much of what follows to Philip Wagner, pioneering grower, winemaker, nurseryman, and author. We can, following Wagner, make a general distinction between two types of climate—mediterranean and continental. The so-called mediterranean climate is characterized by two seasons. A long, hot, arid summer, and a cool, but not cold, rainy winter. In contrast, the continental climate has four distinct seasons. The short summers are hot, and long winters are cold. The mediterranean climate is more or less settled, while the continental climate is unpredictable, with sometimes rapid and extreme fluctuations. Unlike the mediterranean pattern, precipitation occurs in every season.

In the U.S., California has a mediterranean climate, while New England weather is legendary for its changeability. For example . . . late May, 1977: blooming lilacs bow low, under a thick blanket of wet snow . . . Christmas, 1980: an arctic front blasts through the region, and a balmy 50-degree afternoon gives way to a polar night. The thermometer at the base of Hamlet Hill records 20 degrees below zero.

What does this say about the quality of our wine grapes? To answer that question, just take a look at that birthday present your family presented to "the wine lover." I refer here, of course, to that handsomely framed map of the wine regions of Europe, hanging disconsolately on the north wall of your wine cellar. In brief, the warm regions of France, Spain, and Italy have climates that truly deserve the name mediterranean. In contrast, places like Burgundy, Champagne, and the Rhine are situated in the continental zone.

Fine wines from a cool climate

Bowing once again in the general direction of Philip Wagner, I would like to point out that most of the great wines of Europe come from continental, not mediterranean vineyards. The mediterranean climate zones are suitable for producing sweet wines (some of which are delicious) and jug wines—inexpensive, generic wines sold in large containers. Year after year mediterranean vineyards produce huge crops of grapes high in sugar and low in acid. Only in the continental zone, where winters are cold and summers short, do we meet with truly great table wines, made from small crops of grapes perfectly balanced in sugar and acid. Of course, these perfect grapes don't make their appearance every single year. In the continental zones some seasons are too wet or too dry, too cold or too hot or too short for optimum ripeness. In a cold, wet year, even the most famous vineyards can yield a mediocre wine. But in a favorable growing season, continental-zone wines can outshine anything produced in a mediterranean climate.

At the risk of alienating my California friends, I must point out that most California vineyards are located in mediterranean regions where the weather is too hot to produce the finest of wines. Yes, grapevines will flourish in Fresno, producing 10 tons to the acre every year. But those grapes will never yield fine wine. The best California wine comes from regions where the fierce summer heat is tempered by cooling ocean breezes. Even fruit from places like Napa and Sonoma tends to be too high in sugar and low in acid unless it is picked early, before full ripeness—a trick learned only in the last 20 years. The best California wines are good indeed. By planting in the cooler regions, by harvesting early, by machine picking at night when the grapes are cool, it is possible to compensate for California's mediterranean climate.

New England, with its strongly continental climate, can never hope to produce high yields from its vineyards. The vines will not luxuriate as they do in milder climes but must instead spend much of their energy on preparing for winter. Much like vineyards in Burgundy, Champagne, and the Rhine, New England vineyards can ripen only a small crop. But in a really fine year, our vines can produce classically superb wine grapes. Of course, this discussion of mediterranean versus continental climate necessarily involves some oversimplifications and generalities. But I'll stick by my claim: The best harvests of New England can outshine the best of California. If there are challengers to this claim, let them meet me at sundown with an open bottle of California wine. We'll trade toasts at 10 paces (glassware of your choice).

Coastal vineyards get an edge on the weather

In New England the climate pretty well determines where vineyards can be established. In many areas the winter is too severe and the summer too short to ripen a crop of grapes. The best sites are those where the weather is modified by some tempering factor. For example, some vineyards in Massachussetts, Connecticut, and Rhode Island are located near the ocean. The ocean water slows down any changes in temperature and keeps those changes from becoming extreme.

Consider again the 1980 Christmas cold wave. When that arctic air hit the coast, it came into contact with 35-degree ocean water, which was something like 55 degrees warmer than the air. As a result, the frigid air was warmed and the temperature did not plummet as low as it did in more inland areas. (Let's say minus 10 degrees instead of minus 20.) This 10-degree tempering effect could spell the difference between vine survival and disaster. In a winter

cold snap then, the ocean exerts a mollifying influence on the local climate.

A similar effect occurs during the growing season. On a clear, cold night in mid September, for example, inland temperatures might drop below 28 degrees, killing the vine leaves and thus ending the growing season. Time to harvest, whether the grapes are ripe or not. Pity the poor winemaker in this situation. The 16-hours-a-day, 7-days-a-week pace suddenly accelerates to an around-the-clock battle. The enemies? Time and fruit flies. At this point the weather, obeying Murphy's Law, often turns infuriatingly warm—perfect ripening weather after a killing frost.

Let us leave this sad scene and turn our attention back to the coastal vineyard on that same frosty autumn evening. The ocean waters, which have soaked up excess heat all summer long, are now at 65 degrees. They warm the chilly air and keep the vines from losing their leaves. Spared this early frost, the coastal vines might keep their leaves for another month before the next frost finally puts an end to the growing season. Not only does this extra time produce superior fruit, but it leaves the vines in better shape to withstand the winter. Look at it this way.

In a cold climate, vines need to ripen not only the fruit, but the wood as well. Poorly ripened canes will not survive winter cold.

Other ways to beat the odds: lakes and hillsides

As you can see, sites near the shore tend to have favorable climates for winegrowing. But what if you don't happen to own land in Newport, Stonington, or Cape Cod? Are there other factors that might temper the climate enough to permit wine grapes to flourish? There are indeed. For one thing, decent-sized lakes can act as mini oceans in tempering the climate. Of course, if the lake freezes over, it won't be much help in a winter cold snap. But its warm September waters will work to ward off an early frost. This will lengthen the growing season and so allow the vines to "harden off" their wood for winter. They'll stand a better chance of surviving those cold snaps than the vines planted just over the hill, down in a valley with no lake at the bottom.

Another tempering factor may come as a surprise. Have you ever noticed that New England orchards are often located on a hillside? The reason has to do with air drainage. Let's go back to our frosty night in mid September. On the coldest nights the air is still and calm. (We're not talking about wind chill, but low temperatures on the thermometer.) Under these calm conditions, the coldest air, which is denser than warm air, settles downward. It behaves almost like a liquid, collecting in the low spots (frost pockets), and filling valleys. On windy nights the cold and warm air are mixed, and so the valley bottom and hilltop have similar temperatures. But on our clear cold September night, the coldest air is gently collecting in the valley, while the warmer air ends up above it. A valley vineyard might easily suffer a killing frost that night, while high on the hillside, the temperature might stay above 35 degrees. The hillside location allows the cold air to drain off, tempering the climate and lengthening the growing season.

In winter the hillside acts the same way during a cold snap. In January 1982 or 1983 (I forget which), we recorded a frosty 13 degrees below zero on top of Hamlet Hill. On that same night a thermometer at the base of the hill, only half a mile distant, recorded 28 degrees below! The vineyard on the hillside withstood the minus-13-

degree night in fine shape, while the vines at the base of the hill were damaged or destroyed by a temperature 15 degrees lower. The lesson: Never plant in a frost pocket.

Choosing the right hillside is not just a matter of slope, however. Another factor to consider is the aspect or exposure of the site. Hillsides sloping toward the south will receive the most direct sunlight. Vineyards located on a south-, southeast- or southwest-facing slope will therefore be at an advantage. Vines in these locations grow faster in spring and ripen earlier in the fall. A north-facing slope will be relatively shaded and relatively cooler throughout the year. Even natural forest growth testifies to this difference in climate. Often the south slope of a New England hill is covered in oak and maple forest, while on the colder north side, birch and poplar predominate.

To sum up, it is climate that really determines where New England vineyards are located. Several characteristics make for favorable vineyard sites, but, in each case, what growers look for is some tempering factor. In our climate this means something to lengthen the growing season and/or soften the harsh winter cold.

The ancient and vulnerable vinifera

So far in talking about climate, I've referred only to vines and vineyards, with no mention of specific varieties of grapes. Fortunately, while it is true that climate limits which varieties can be grown in New England, there is still a considerable latitude of choice. There are 20 or so varieties of wine grapes grown in our region. Broadly speaking, they fall into two groups—vinifera and hybrids. The first group includes the classical grapes of antiquity. When Plato and the Bible mention wine, they're talking vinifera. Familiar vinifera varieties grown in New England include Riesling, Chardonnay, Pinot Noir, Cabernet Sauvignon, and Gewurztraminer. Some less familiar varieties are Pinot Meunier, Cabernet Franc, and Muscadet.

The hybrids, on the other hand, have a history going back some 100 years. At that time an obscure insect called phylloxera began devastating vineyards in France. This aphid was accidentally introduced from eastern North America where it had quietly evolved in harmony with native grapevines for untold eons. When phylloxera feeds on our native grapevines, their measured response is to shrug off the damage and simply heal the small wound made by the insect. When phylloxera began feeding on the vinifera vineyards of Bordeaux, however, their response was more dramatic. The vines weakened and died. Much like an isolated island population devastated by the measles virus, the vinifera vines of the Old World had never developed immunity to the suddenly deadly insect.

One response by the people of France was an upwelling of anti-American sentiment whose faint echoes may still be heard today. Visiting a St. Emilion chateau in 1971, I was a bit taken aback when the owner, an otherwise hospitable gentleman, looked at me accusingly and said, "The phylloxera came from America, you know."

The hybrid: a constructive response

A more constructive response to the phylloxera invasion was the creation of thousands of hybrid grapevines. Hybridizers such as Seibel, Ravat, Baco, and Seyve-Villard spent long years crossing native American grapes with viniferas and evaluating the hybrid offspring. They sought vines that combined the phylloxera resistance of the American varieties with the wine quality of the old world viniferas. Of the many thousands of crosses made, only a few dozen were truly successful. Some of these hybrid varieties, imported 50 years ago by Philip Wagner, are suited to the New England climate. A tour through our vineyards will find varieties with names like Baco Noir, Foch, Chancellor, Vidal, Ravat, Aurora, and Cascade.

Both hybrids and viniferas have their champions. In the vineyard, vinifera varieties are harder to grow. They tend to be less cold resistant and more disease prone than the hybrids mentioned above. Also, the vinifera varieties require grafting onto special rootstocks. (These rootstocks are themselves hybrids and were developed to withstand attacks by phylloxera.) The hybrids can be grown upon their own roots. They tend to be cold hardy and tend (with specific exceptions) to be less prone to disease than vinifera vines. A logical choice for siting a vinifera vineyard would be close to the shore where the climate is relatively mild. The hardier hybrids are useful for sites with less forgiving winters.

Vine personalities

In addition to these general characteristics, each hybrid and each vinifera variety has its own unique vineyard personality. Baco Noir, for example, is extremely vigorous and must be pruned so as to leave many buds—this helps to control excess vigor. Chancellor, in contrast, tends to be a compact vine and must be pruned back severely to prevent excessive crop load. Cabernet Sauvignon is relatively hardy for a vinifera but requires a long season to ripen the fruit and avoid a "green" taste in the wine. Foch ripens early and can be grown on sites that have a short season due to early frost. Muscadet holds promise as a cold-hardy white vinifera. To my mind this wine resembles Chardonnay, and it is one of my personal favorites. Because we get more summer heat than cloudy western France, our Muscadet will taste like no other. So far it is grown here only in experimental amounts. Another interesting experiment is Philip Wagner's White Rogue, a hybrid of unknown parentage. It stowed away, masquerading as a red grape in some of Wagner's original shipments from France. This variety has proven to be extremely cold hardy and disease resistant. It ripens even earlier than Aurora. It is hoped that enough of the wine will be made to evaluate White Rogue's potential in the next few years.

Because New England is a relatively young wine region, we are still in the process of matching sites to varieties. The future is wide open, and exciting discoveries lie ahead.

New England soil: a legacy of the ice age

So far, we've taken a look at the region's climate and at some of the varieties of grapes suited to various types of vineyard sites. But what of the New England soil? Is it suitable for vineyard culture? Isn't that what determines the difference between wine regions?

Though I hate to fly in the face of tradition, I don't believe soil type has much influence in determining wine character. I won't deny that there can be a subtle difference between wines from various soils. Baco Noir from eastern Connecticut seems more delicate in flavor than the same variety grown in the Finger Lakes of New York. *Maybe* this is a result of the different soil changing the character of the wine. But overall, climate and variety are far more important. Don't misunderstand me. Soil type can have a drastic influence on vine growth. But this generally comes down to a matter of vine vigor. Grapevines thrive on well-drained soils. Plant Seyval on a deep, gravelly loam, and you'll get large vines that can yield a consistent five or six tons per acre. Put the same Seyval on heavy clay, and you'll get what looks like a different variety. The small compact vines will bear no more than two or three tons. These are the sorts of differences caused by soil type.

Because of New England's recent glacial scouring, our

soils may vary drastically even within one small vineyard plot. For example, a Massachusetts hillside crushed by a mile-high ice sheet has a compressed hardpan layer almost like rock. The Pinot Noir vines that grow there are small; their roots are unable to penetrate the hardpan. Right next to this hardpan patch, a gravelly area marks the spot where, 10,000 years ago, a river poured out of the glacier as it melted back. The swift-moving water washed all fine clay particles downstream. Only larger particles were heavy enough to settle at this point. The vines send their roots deep into the porous gravel and are large and vigorous.

Suppose we make two batches of Pinot Noir. One comes from the small hardpan vines, the other from the vigorous gravel-bank vines. Will they taste different? Perhaps. But if you trucked in a thousand tons of Napa Valley gravel bank and dumped it on the Massachusetts hillside, the vines would grow vigorously in the gravel. If you made wine from those vines, what would it taste like? Would it taste like a cross between a Napa Pinot and a Massachusetts Pinot? Absolutely not. It would taste exactly like a Pinot Noir from Massachusetts. If you won't take my word for it, you are welcome to try the experiment yourself.

What *is* a New England wine?

This raises an interesting question. What does a Massachussetts Pinot Noir taste like? A thorough discussion of the different New England wines would, of course, occupy many pages. But a few general words are in order. First, I would say that our regional whites tend to be light and, for want of a better word, snappy. Bitter tannins are low in New England reds. Both of these characteristics are common to wines from this type of climate. In good years our wines have plenty of fruit. The most fragrant Riesling I've ever tasted was grown in western Connecticut. (It was a homemade wine.)

I'd also like to add a few words on the controversy of vinifera versus hybrid wines. Some vinifera fanciers claim that all hybrid wines have a "foxy" taste. They are referring to the taste of Niagara and Concord grapes (the Welch's grape juice taste). My own experience tells me that only a very few of the hybrids have this flavor. In 1974, while I was cellarmaster at Bully Hill, in New York state, I climbed into a redwood tank that had just been emptied of 3,000 gallons of wine. (No, I didn't get a buzz.) The wine was from a hybrid variety called Rougeon. I clearly remember the slight Concord-like fragrance in the tank. (A good winemaker has a hound dog's nose and an elephant's memory.) Most hybrids have no such foxy character at all.

Each hybrid is different—as different from one another as Riesling is from Chardonnay. This is only to be expected, since each hybrid has a unique and complex parentage. Those who lump all the hybrids together with a sniff of derision are guilty of a kind of viticultural racism. The best hybrid wines, like the best viniferas, are worthy of admiration, even to the point of consumption (the sincerest form of admiration). A well-made Seyval is superior to a mediocre Chardonnay or Riesling. And some longtime admirers of Beaujolais Nouveau would be shocked to discover that the wine they impatiently crave is often an under-the-table blend of vinifera and hybrid.

A toast to a new industry

The New England wine industry is still in its infancy, with only a 20-year history. In that short span of time, several million bottles of regional wine have been produced. The wine in those bottles has faithfully borne with it the character of New England's vineyards. I'll end as I began, by raising a glass of 1984 Riesling. Here's a toast: May the public and the critics give New England wine the credit it's due.

If I forgot to mention it, the Riesling in question took first prize at the 1986 San Francisco County Fair.

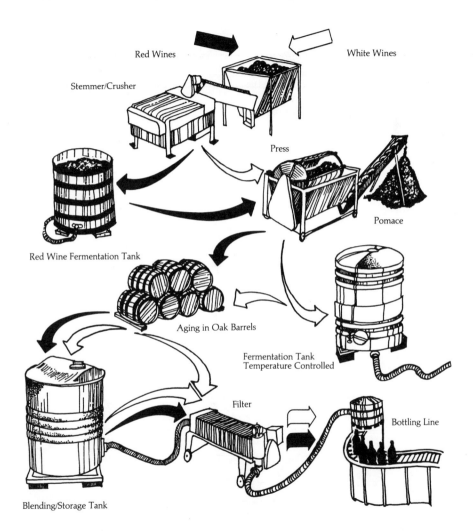

Red Wines

White Wines

Stemmer/Crusher

Press

Pomace

Red Wine Fermentation Tank

Aging in Oak Barrels

Fermentation Tank
Temperature Controlled

Filter

Bottling Line

Blending/Storage Tank

THE WINE-MAKING PROCESS: Black and white arrows indicate the steps in producing wines from red and white grapes.

New England fruit wines: A primer

by Jack Partridge

NEW ENGLAND IS FAMOUS FOR the quality and flavor of its apples, blueberries, cranberries, and other fruits. If those fruits could only produce wine, what wine it would be.

Well, they can, and it is. In fact, New England is rapidly becoming premium fruit-wine country. More than a dozen wineries are now producing high-quality wines from native New England fruits.

Our hats are off to those who have learned to grow fine wine grapes in our unpredictable region. But we have demonstrated here in New England that fruit wines need make no apologies to the grape. Properly made, fruit wines can be just as appealing as grape wines for aperitif, dinner, or dessert. And they introduce a whole new range of flavors to the fine-wine experience. Why fruit wines?

But wait, you say, doesn't fruit wine mean Boone's Farm and sticky-sweet Kosher wines, pop wines, and novelties? Unfortunately, that's what most commercial fruit wines have been. But that has little to do with what fruit wines can be.

Fruit wines can be sweet or bone dry. They can be full

JACK PARTRIDGE started Nashoba Valley Winery in 1978. A city planner at the time, he had been making wine as a hobby and was impressed with the wines that could be made from native New England fruits. After starting out in West Concord, the winery was moved to its permanent home in a 55-acre "winery orchard" in Bolton, Massachusetts.

flavored or delicate. They can be simple and fruity or complex and sophisticated. They can be excellent or downright awful. In other words, fruit wines are capable of the same range of virtues and vices as grape wines. Why fruit wines? The proper answer is why not?

Fruit wines suffer mainly from an image problem. Many people have tasted bad fruit wines; few people have tasted good ones. In our tasting room, for instance, the most common reaction is one of surprise: "Oh, but this is a good wine. I had no idea!" All that is slowly changing as more and more people are exposed to good fruit wines. Our New England fruit wines are winning medals in national wine competitions. They are being sold in most good wine stores in New England and in some outside the region. They are appearing on the wine lists of more and more fine restaurants. Premium fruit wines are becoming a New England specialty.

What is fruit wine and how is it made?

Fruit wine is wine made from fruits other than grapes. In practice the term sometimes includes all non-grape wine, including such things as honey wine (mead), rhubarb wine, dandelion wine, etc. Most fruits can be used for wine. Some seem to work better than others, but it is hard to think of a fruit from which wine cannot or has not been made.

The production of fruit wine is quite similar to that of grape wine. Wine yeasts ferment the fruit juice. Reds wines are usually pulp fermented, whites usually juice fermented. The wines need aging, and either barrels or tanks can be used, depending on the style desired. Most of the traditional winemaking practices apply to fruit wine-making: selection of fruit for quality and level of ripeness, choice of yeast strains, cleanliness, temperature control, blending, judicious filtering and fining, etc.

But there are differences. The process of crushing and pressing the fruits varies considerably from the treatment of grapes. Apples and pears must be ground up or pulverized before pressing. Peaches must be removed from their stones. Other fruits present special challenges depending on their size and shape and the nature of the pulp and skin. Learning how to deal with each fruit and how different treatments affect wine characteristics is part of the adventure of commercial fruit winemaking. There is still a lot to learn.

Another difference is that fruit wines afford more flexibility in the timing of production. Grapes must be crushed in the fall when they are ripe. We find that the same applies to some fruits, such as peaches. But other fruits like apples and pears can be kept for months in cold storage, allowing us to spread out the production season. We even prefer to use some fruits frozen. And so it's possible to be pressing wines every month of the year.

A third difference is that few fruits have the sugar level of the grape. Since that sugar level determines the alcohol level of the wine, we must add sugar at fermentation to produce the desired amount of alcohol. With fruit wine, chaptalisation—the addition of sugar—is standard.

Finally, most fruit wines require less aging than grape wines. We age most of our wines three to six months in tank or barrel, and for some, little further bottle aging is required. One prominent exception is blueberry wine, which behaves more like a typical red grape wine, developing and changing over several years of bottle aging. When young, it has a clean, fresh character with recognizable blueberry "fruit" (the flavors and aromas of the source fruit). After several years it is often taken for a grape wine, with somewhat of a Bordeaux character.

Fruit wine is food wine

Fruit wines are great food wines. They have the structure to match just about any dish, and they bring a wider range of flavors to the meal than grape wines. Some fruit wines have flavor and style characteristics which are entirely new to the food and wine experience.

Some combinations are suggested by the fruits themselves. For example, fresh pears and Brie make a superb combination, and we find pear wine an excellent accompaniment to that cheese. Similarly, a good apple wine goes nicely with pork. And for those who still do not know it, cranberry-apple is *the* wine to have with turkey. Here the food and wine combination draws on the traditional cranberry-turkey connection embedded in our senses from countless Thanksgiving dinners. And the deep rose color of the wine adds a festive note to the holiday table.

Other combinations are not so obvious but are no less effective. Apple wine is often very light and delicate. Such a wine is a perfect match for some salads. Blueberry wine, on the other hand, can be quite full flavored and robust. It is excellent with lamb and beef, as well as with duck, goose, and game.

Peach wine happens to combine a generous fruit flavor and aroma with full body and a high level of acidity. Finished as a dessert wine it is a unique sensory combination—at once sweet, flavorful, and tartly refreshing. We find it makes an excellent after-dinner drink, either by itself or matched with fruits, chocolate, or many other desserts.

Because most people are new to fruit wines, we have developed a food and wine chart for our own wines. This chart indicates some of the food and wine matches which we and our customers have found pleasing. The chart can also be used with other New England fruit wines, given some knowledge of styles, sweetness levels, etc. However, as we say on the chart, there are no hard and fast rules in matching wine to foods. Let your taste buds be your ultimate guide.

Exploring a new territory

The grape wine industry has developed over a period of centuries, with countless experiments often extending decades. Particular kinds of grapes were grown on a particular site, vinified with particular winemaking techniques. Along the way many indifferent wines were produced, but from that long series of experiments emerged the great wines of the world.

In those terms the fruit wine industry is still in its infancy. We know we can make some very good wines, but we don't really know what the full potential is. We are still exploring different fruits and varieties, still learning the basics of how to handle each fruit. And we have hardly begun to assess the influence of site, soil, and fruit-growing practices on ultimate wine quality.

From the winemaker's point of view, one of the most exciting things about fruit wines in New England is the exploration—all that remains to be discovered. For the wine lover, there is already an abundance of good wine to be tasted, and the adventure of all the new food and wine possibilities.

Everyone with a real interest in wine owes it to him- or herself to go out and learn about the new generation of fruit wines. New England fruit wines offer a fascinating new wine territory. Do help us explore it.

FACING PAGE: This chart gives suggestions on what Nashoba Valley wines to try with different foods, but you can use it for ideas on how other kinds of fruit wines might complement a meal.

FOOD & WINE CHART
NASHOBA VALLEY WINERY

KEY:
★ Perfect Match   ● Highly Recommended   ▲ Gourmet Adventure

		GRAVENSTEIN	BALDWIN	DRY PEAR	UPLAND WHITE	MAIDEN'S BLUSH	CYSER	CRANBERRY-APPLE	DRY BLUEBERRY	UPLAND RED	SEMI-SWT BLUEBERRY	PLUM	AFTER DINNER PEACH	STRAWBERRY	RASPBERRY
Aperitif	Wine for sipping by itself	●	★	★	★	★	●	★	★	●	●	★	★	●	★
	Mild cheeses	★	★	★	●	★	▲	●							
	Strong cheeses	▲	▲	▲	▲	●	▲	●	★	★	●	▲	▲	▲	
	Mild flavored dips	●	●	●	●	●	▲								
	Spicy dips and appetizers	▲	▲	▲	▲	●		★	●	●	●	●	●	▲	
	Oysters, cherrystones, etc.	★	●	●	★	●									
Lighter Main Courses	Mild-flavored vegetarian	★	★	●	●	●			▲						
	Pasta, white sauce	●	●	●	●	●									
	Mild-flavored oriental dishes	●	●	★	●	●	▲								
	Mild-flavored seafood dishes	●	★	★	●	●									
	Mild-flavored poultry dishes	★	●	●	★	★									
	Veal, white sauce	★	●	●	●	●			▲						
Hearty Main Courses	Roast turkey	●	●	▲	●	●	●	▲	★	●	●	▲	▲		
	Ham	▲	▲	▲	▲	●	▲		★	▲	▲	▲	●	▲	
	Roast pork	●	●	▲	▲	●	●	●	▲	▲					
	Roast beef, lamb								▲	★	★	▲			
	Pasta, red sauce					●			▲	●	★	▲			
	Hot, spicy "ethnic dishes"	●	●	▲	▲	●			★						
Desserts	Wine in place of dessert							▲		●	★	★	★	★	
	Cakes, cookies, pastries						▲				●	★	★	●	
	Fruits						▲				▲	★	★	★	★
	Dessert cheeses						●	▲			★	★	●	●	●
	Icecream												●	●	●
	Chocolate dishes												●	●	★

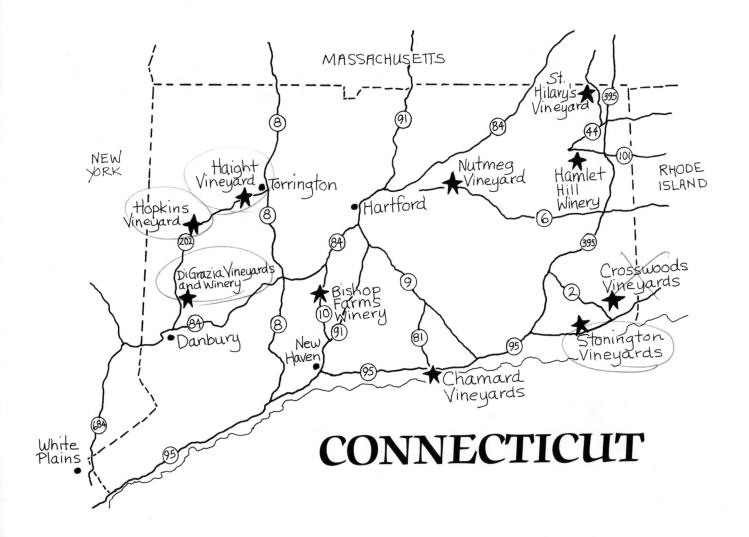

MASSACHUSETTS

NEW YORK

St. Hilary's Vineyard

395

44

Nutmeg Vineyard

Hamlet Hill Winery

101

RHODE ISLAND

Haight Vineyard

Torrington

Hopkins Vineyard

202

Hartford

6

8

91

84

DiGrazia Vineyards and Winery

Bishop Farms Winery

10

9

84

Danbury

8

395

Crosswoods Vineyards

2

Stonington Vineyards

91

81

New Haven

95

95

Chamard Vineyards

684

White Plains

95

CONNECTICUT

The BISHOP FARMS Inc.
Better Fruits

BISHOP'S APPLE WINE

Contains
Sulfites

Alcohol 11%
By Volume
FW-13
CT-W-15

CONNECTICUT GROWN

PRODUCED
and
BOTTLED
by
BISHOP FARMS, INC.
500 So. Meriden RD.
Cheshire, CT

Acres of apple blossoms are a spring attraction of Bishop Farms, but there's much to see and do in other seasons too.

Bishop Farms Winery

THE BISHOP FAMILY HAS BEEN growing fruit and pressing cider for nearly a century, but since 1987, Bishop Farms has also produced fruit wine. This new venture came after two years of working to obtain the necessary state and federal permits that made Bishop Farms the first farm winery in Connecticut to produce only fruit wine. The Bishops are joined in their enterprise by Pomp Lentini, winemaker and former wine-equipment-store owner.

Fruit acreage consists of apples, peaches, pears, plums, and small fruits such as raspberries, blueberries, as well as table grapes.

Visitors to Bishop Farms can tour the winery, pick fruit, and taste the Bishop's fruit wines. Picnic areas are available at the farm, and children can pet and feed the donkeys, Pigmy goats, chickens, geese, ducks, and an assortment of rabbits.

500 South Meriden Road
Cheshire, CT 06410
203-272-8243

ESTABLISHED: 1987
OWNERS: John and Kathleen Bishop
ACRES: 10
OUTPUT: 700 gallons
VISITING: Open daily 10-5, August through December, March to June.
DIRECTIONS: In central Connecticut between Interstates 91 and 84, on Routes 70 and 68.

WINES:
Sweet Apple
Dry Apple
Pear
Cranberry-Apple

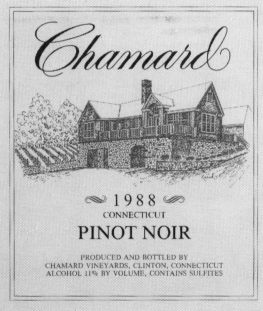

Chamard Vineyards

PURSUING AN INTEREST IN FARMING and fine wines, the Chaney family established the Chamard Vineyards in 1983. The vineyard's site was chosen for its proximity to Long Island Sound, which affords a longer growing season and less variable temperatures than found elsewhere in New England. The Chaneys cleared the wooded land and planted 15 acres of vinifera grapes, experimenting and growing for several years before their first harvest in 1986. Their first commercial wine release was in 1989. The vineyard's rich, stony soil combines with the climate to produce optimum growing conditions for their European-style wines. Winemaker Larry McCulloch came to Chamard with an agriculture degree from Ohio State and with winemaking experience from vineyards in the Hudson Valley region of New York.

The new winery was built with fieldstones from the Chaney property and wooden beams milled from trees from the vineyard's land. Its classic New England design is combined with modern winemaking equipment, including jacketed stainless steel tanks and French oak barrels used to age the wines.

Chamard Vineyards is located in a historic area of Connecticut, close to the Connecticut River and popular vacation spots. There is a nearby state park with picnic facilities.

115 Cow Hill Road
Clinton, CT 06413
203-664-0299

ESTABLISHED: 1983
OWNERS: the Chaney family
ACRES: 15 planted
OUTPUT: 15,000 gallons
VISITING: Tours and tastings by appointment only.
DIRECTIONS: Take exit 63 off Interstate 95 and go north on Route 81 for .25 mile. Turn left on Walnut Hill Road, which becomes Cow Hill Road. The winery's stone gate is approximately 1 mile up on Cow Hill Road.

WINES:
Chardonnay
Cabernet Sauvignon
Pinot Noir

1986

CROSSWOODS

RESSLER VINEYARDS

NORTH FORK, LONG ISLAND, NY

MERLOT

PRODUCED AND BOTTLED BY
CROSSWOODS VINEYARDS, INC. NORTH STONINGTON, CT 06359
BONDED WINERY NO. CT 22, ALCOHOL 12.5% BY VOLUME
CONTAINS SULFITES

Susan Connell studied wine science and apprenticed at a vineyard before she and her husband founded Cross-woods. Though some grapes are bought from nearby Long Island, Crosswoods' award-winning Chardonnay is a Connecticut product.

Crosswoods Vineyards

THIS 433-ACRE CONNECTICUT FARM overlooking the Atlantic Ocean is the birthplace of what has been described as some of the best Chardonnnay in the country. Crosswoods Vineyards' Chardonnay was among the 50 American wines to be served at the Gala Food, Wine and Lager Festival, one of the special events following the inauguration of President George Bush.

In 1988, Crosswoods president and general manager Susan Connell was named the Les Amis du Vin "wineperson of the year," the first woman to receive the award. Her husband Hugh Connell, a retired lawyer, is the secretary and treasurer of the vineyard. The Connells, New York natives, created the vineyard together, planting their first vines and hiring a winemaker in 1981.

Despite a longstanding contention by some wine experts that growing vinifera grapes is impossible in New England, Susan Connell and her husband believe that the ocean climate at Crosswoods is like the climate of Bordeaux, France. They feel that coastal New England's fairly long ripening time produces a full-tasting wine.

With the guidance of California-educated winemaker George Sulick, the Connell family and their staff produce a number of wines from their own grapes as well as from grapes sent by ferry from the Ressler Vineyard on Long Island.

75 Chester Maine Road
North Stonington, CT 06359
203-535-2205

ESTABLISHED: 1981
OWNERS: Susan and Hugh Connell
ACRES: 35
OUTPUT: 7,000 cases
VISITING: Open daily. Tours and tastings Saturday and Sunday 12-5. Large groups call ahead.
DIRECTIONS: From Interstate 95 go west on Route 2, following the vineyard signs. Crosswoods is approximately 3 miles from the interstate.

WINES:
Chardonnnay (estate)
Chardonnay (Ressler Vineyards)
Merlot (Ressler)
Gamay Noir (estate)
Scrimshaw White

closed out of business lovely old farm house & barn

BLACKSMITH
An American port

DiGrazia
VINEYARDS

Honey Blush

a demi-sec
wine made from honey
vatted with fermented

NEWBURY
A nouveau red wine

DiGrazia
VINEYARDS

PRODUCED AND BOTTLED BY
DiGrazia Vineyards and Winery
BROOKFIELD CENTER, CONNECTICUT
ALCOHOL 11.5% BY VOLUME
CONTAINS SULFITES

FIELDSTONE RESERVE
A red wine

DiGrazia
VINEYARDS

PRODUCED AND BOTTLED BY
DiGrazia Vineyards and Winery
BROOKFIELD CENTER, CONNECTICUT
ALCOHOL 11.5% BY VOLUME
CONTAINS SULFITES

MEADOWBROOK
A white wine

DiGrazia
VINEYARDS

PRODUCED AND BOTTLED BY
DiGrazia Vineyards and Winery
BROOKFIELD CENTER, CONNECTICUT
ALCOHOL 11.5% BY VOLUME
CONTAINS SULFITES

DiGrazia Vineyards and Winery

GROWING GRAPES BEGAN AS A hobby for Dr. Paul DiGrazia. After attending medical school in Switzerland, where he became fascinated with local vineyards, Dr. DiGrazia and his wife Barbara began experimenting with vinifera vines. These were eventually replaced by hardier French-American hybrids, and by 1978 the DiGrazia vineyards were in full swing. The winery, initially housed in the DiGrazias' garage, was started in 1984. It currently produces 10 wines, made exclusively from the DiGrazias' own grapes.

Since its inception, DiGrazia wines have won 18 medals in regional, national, and international wine competitions. In January of 1990, Dr. DiGrazia was named Connecticut Wineperson of the Year by the Eastern Connecticut Chapter of Les Amis du Vin.

The DiGrazia Vineyards and Winery combines traditional winemaking methods with ultra-modern American equipment and technology. The DiGrazias continue to experiment with winemaking techniques, including using honey instead of sulfites for anti-oxidation in their wine processing. Their Honey Blush is made without preservatives, and the DiGrazias use organic fungicides and mechanical methods of weed control where possible.

The winery was featured on the TV show, *Robin Leach's Lifestyles of the Rich and Famous*, in which soap-opera actress Linda Danho claimed DiGrazia's Wind Ridge was better than chateau-bottled or California wines. As reported in the *New England Wine Gazette*, Ms. Danho stated, "Look out Napa Valley. Connecticut is coming. Connecticut is coming."

131 Tower Road
Brookfield Center, CT 06804
203-775-1616

ESTABLISHED: 1984
OWNER: Dr. Paul DiGrazia
ACRES: 55
OUTPUT: 7,500 gallons
VISITING: Saturday and Sunday 11-5, January through March. Tuesday through Sunday 11-5, April through December. Guided tours and free tastings.
DIRECTIONS: 1 mile east of the intersection of Routes 133 and 25 in Brookfield Center. From Route 84, take exit 9, follow Route 25 north to Brookfield Center, go 1 mile east on Route 133.

WINES:
Blacksmith
Heritage
Newbury
Fieldstone Reserve
Candlewood
Honey Blush
Anastasia's Blush
Meadowbrook Classic
Meadowbrook
Wind Ridge
✓ VIDAL BLANC LATE HARVEST

Sherman Haight displays some of his winery's products, with part of the vineyard in the background.

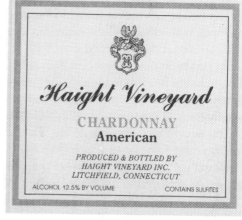

Haight Vineyard

LITCHFIELD, CONNECTICUT—HOME TO HARRIET Beecher Stowe, Henry Ward Beecher, and Oliver Wolcott, Jr.—is also the site of the Haight Vineyard. Owner and founder Sherman Haight, who says he was a frustrated farmer with an interest in fine wines, began experimenting with grape growing in 1970. He didn't know then if his vines would survive in the cold climate of the Connecticut highlands, or if the grapes would produce enough sugar for successful winemaking. Since 1978, however, Haight Vineyards has grown a small number of varieties suited to fine winemaking, including Chardonnay, Riesling, Seyval Blanc, and Marechal Foch. These vines have adapted well to the vineyard's air-drained slopes, cool growing temperatures, and 1,100-foot altitude. The vineyard grows all of its own grapes. Haight is joined by winemaker Charles Flatt.

Since its inception in 1978, the winery has been successful in wine competitions. The Haight Riesling won the Best of Class and the gold medal at the prestigious Wineries Unlimited competition. The Marechal Foch took a silver medal, and the Haight Chardonnay won the bronze.

The main building at Haight Vineyards is the new Tudor winery. It contains an outside pressing deck, wine cellars, aging rooms, and the winery's comfortable tasting room. Visitors to Haight Vineyards are encouraged to take the popular Vineyard Walk, a self-guided tour through the rows of grape vines. The historic town of Litchfield is visible from parts of the vineyard, and picnic tables are available.

29 Chestnut Hill Road
Litchfield, CT 06759
203-567-4045

ESTABLISHED: 1975
OWNER: Sherman P. Haight, Jr.
ACRES: 35
OUTPUT: 70 tons
VISITING: Open Monday through Saturday 10:30-5, Sundays 12-5, year round. Continuous tastings and free tours.
DIRECTIONS: 1 mile east of Litchfield on Chestnut Hill Road, off Route 118.

WINES:
Covertside White
Barely Blush
Chestnut Hill White
Marechal Foch
Chardonnay
Riesling
Recolte
Méthode Champenoise
Sparkling Wine

HAMLET HILL

NEW ENGLAND
Autumn Blush

A PREMIER CONNECTICUT ROSÉ WINE

ALCOHOL 12% BY VOLUME

PRODUCED AND BOTTLED BY
The Hamlet Hill Wines Co.
POMFRET, CONNECTICUT 06258

HAMLET HILL

CONNECTICUT

SEYVAL BLANC
Vintage 1986

A PREMIER CONNECTICUT WHITE WINE

ALCOHOL 12% BY VOLUME

PRODUCED AND BOTTLED BY
The Hamlet Hill Wines Co.
POMFRET, CONNECTICUT 06258

HAMLET HILL

1986 VINTAGE

DRY RIESLING

CONNECTICUT — NORTH FORK

ALCOHOL 12% BY VOLUME

PRODUCED AND BOTTLED BY
The Hamlet Hill Wines Co.
POMFRET, CONNECTICUT 06258

Hamlet Hill Winery

HAMLET HILL'S FOUNDER, A.W. LOOS, started growing wine grapes on his northeastern Connecticut land in 1975. Wild grapes seemed to thrive there, Loos had discovered, and he believed the climate was similar to the famous grape-growing regions of Europe. That year he cleared 30 acres of land and planted 5 acres of vines. Half of the grapes planted were Seyve-Villard, a white French hybrid, and the other half were red hybrids, including Marechal Foch, Cascade, Baco, Colobel and Chancellor. The first harvest was in the fall of 1978, and the next year another two acres were planted. There are now 28 acres of vines at Hamlet Hill. In 1986 the winery was sold to Henry Maubert, an international business consultant, and John Spitzer, an advertising executive. The owners work under the guidance of a wine consultant from France.

The building that houses Hamlet Hill Winery was built in 1981, and it is unique. It employs a combination of geo, solar, and ultra-insulation techniques for energy efficiency—both the fermentation and production cellars are set into a hillside—requiring neither heating nor cooling, and maintaining a perfect temperature for maturing the wines.

Post Office Box 45, Route 101
Pomfret, CT 06258
203-928-5550

ESTABLISHED: 1974
FOUNDER: A.W. Loos
OWNERS: Henry J. Maubert and John Spitzer
ACRES: 28
OUTPUT: 20,000 cases
VISITING: Visits and tours daily 10-5. Small groups unscheduled, groups of 12 or more, call ahead.
DIRECTIONS: From Sturbridge, Massachusetts, take 131 south to Southbridge, then 169 south to Pomfret. From Mystic, take 117 north to Norwich, then Route 12 north to 169 north to Pomfret.

WINES:
Seyval Brut
Celebration Harvest
Dry Riesling
Charter Oak Red
Woodstock White
Chardonnay
Autumn Blush

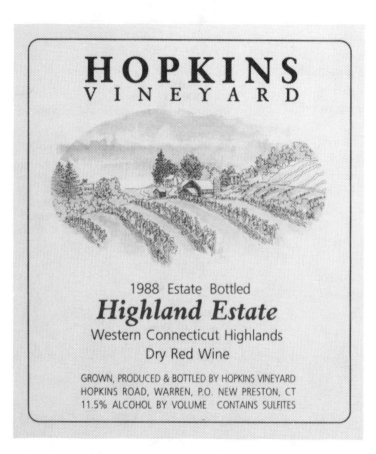

HOPKINS
V I N E Y A R D

1988 Estate Bottled
Highland Estate
Western Connecticut Highlands
Dry Red Wine

GROWN, PRODUCED & BOTTLED BY HOPKINS VINEYARD
HOPKINS ROAD, WARREN, P.O. NEW PRESTON, CT
11.5% ALCOHOL BY VOLUME   CONTAINS SULFITES

HOPKINS VINEYARD

Table Wine
First Blush

PRODUCED & BOTTLED BY HOPKINS VINEYARD, HOPKINS ROAD
WARREN, P.O. NEW PRESTON, CT   12.0% ALCOHOL BY VOLUME

Hopkins Vineyard

HOUSED IN A RENOVATED RED and white barn, the winery of Hopkins Vineyard sits at the top of rolling hills overlooking Lake Waramaug. The farm has been part of the Hopkins family since the signing of the Constitution in 1787, but it wasn't until the past decade that the family joined the New England wine producing community.

In 1979, a year after the Farm Winery Act legalized commercial production of wine in Connecticut, owners William and Judith Hopkins gave up dairy farming to plant their first 20 acres of grapes. The vineyard is located in the Western Highlands viticultural area, which contains some of the oldest rock in Connecticut. As a result of glacial deposits from the last ice age, Hopkins' soil is well-drained sand or gravel, ideal for growing grapes.

Winemaker William Hopkins prides himself on following old-world winemaking techniques. Wine is fermented in tanks and oak barrels in the lower level of the Hopkins' barn and then stored in the basement, kept cool by the surrounding ancient stone walls of the cellar.

Though most of the winery's output is traditional red and white wine from French-American hybrid grapes, the Hopkins also produce hard cider and are currently developing their first batch of sparkling wine.

Hopkins Road in Warren
New Preston, CT 06777
203-868-7954

ESTABLISHED: 1979
OWNERS: Judith and William Hopkins
ACRES: 25
OUTPUT: 7,000 cases
VISITING: Open daily 10-5, May 1 to January 1. Friday, Saturday, and Sunday 10-5, January 2 to April 30. Self-guided tours welcome. Group tours by appointment at $3.50 per person. Tastings every day when open.
DIRECTIONS: Take Route 202 to New Preston, then follow Route 45 north to North Shore Road. Follow signs to the winery on Hopkins Road.

WINES:
Seyval Blanc
Chardonnay
Vineyard Reserve White
Highland Estate
Sachem's Picnic
First Blush
Vignoles
Sauterne
Yankee Cider

NUTMEG VINEYARD

ANTONIO
TOLLAND COUNTY
DRY RED WINE
1982

PRODUCED AND BOTTLED BY ANTHONY ROSARIO M
NUTMEG VINEYARD 800 BUNKER HILL ROAD
COVENTRY, CONNECTICUT BW-CT-19 CONTAINS SU
MAIL: P.O. BOX 146, ANDOVER, CT 06232

NUTMEG VINEYARD

VIDAL BLAN
WHITE WINE
DRY

PRODUCED & BOTTLED BY ANTHONY ROSAR
NUTMEG VINEYARD 800 BUNKER HILL
COVENTRY, CONNECTICUT BW-CT-19 CONTA
MAIL. P.O. BOX 146, ANDOVER, CT 0

NUTMEG VINEYARD

SWEET

13% ALCOHOL
BY VOLUME

BISHOP'S WINE
SPICED RED WINE

MADE FROM GRAPE WINE WITH SPICES
AND NATURAL FLAVORS ADDED
PRODUCED AND BOTTLED BY ANTHONY ROSARIO MAULUCCI
NUTMEG VINEYARD 800 BUNKER HILL ROAD
COVENTRY, CONNECTICUT BW-CT-19 CONTAINS SULFITES
MAIL: P.O. BOX 146, ANDOVER, CT 06232

Nutmeg Vineyard

AT THE AGE OF 30 Tony Maulucci decided to abandon his career as a toolmaker and become a farmer. In 1968 he bought 37.8 acres in Coventry, land that was filled with boulders and trees, and started clearing. His decision to plant grapes was in part a response to the rolling hills and southern exposure of the land, and in 1970 the Maulucci family began their first, experimental plantings. The winery, which Maulucci describes as "primitive, tiny, remote . . . a one-man show," was built and bonded in 1982.

Nutmeg Vineyard uses traditional winemaking techniques, but their wines range from dry white table wines such as Vidal Blanc to sweet dessert wines like American Strawberry or American Raspberry, wines that reflect the region's agriculture. Though the vines are grown on only five acres of the Maulucci's land, a one-time swamp has been turned into a pond, and the remaining acreage is now a well-managed forest. A drive up the scenic road will take visitors back to a less hurried time. They can taste the farm-made wines, chat with Tony Maulucci, and see his antique farm equipment.

800 Bunker Hill Road
Andover, CT 06232
203-742-8402

ESTABLISHED: first plantings 1970, winery 1982
OWNER: Anthony R. Maulucci
ACRES: 5
OUTPUT: 2,000 gallons
VISITING: Open for tours and tastings Saturday and Sunday, 11-5, year round.
DIRECTIONS: From Manchester, go east on Route 6, turn north after the blinking caution lights in Andover onto Bunker Hill Road. The winery is 2 miles up on the left.

WINES:
Seyval
Vidal
Baco Noir
Antonio
Rosario
Raspberry
Strawberry
Peach
Blueberry
Cherry
Angel Wings
Bishop's Wine

Estate Bottled

St. Hilary's

Windham Red
Table Wine

PRODUCED AND BOTTLED BY
ST. HILARY'S VINEYARD, NO. GROSVENORDALE, CT
ALCOHOL CONTENT 12 PERCENT BY VOLUME

Estate Bottled

St. Hilary's

Golden Muscat

PRODUCED AND BOTTLED BY:
ST. HILARY'S VINEYARD, NO. GROSVENORDALE, CT
ALCOHOL CONTENT 12 PERCENT BY VOLUME

The oldest farm winery in Connecticut, St. Hilary's is appropriately housed in a more than 200-year-old building.

St. Hilary's Vineyard

SET ON A HILL AND encompassing 44 acres of crops and forests, St. Hilary's Vineyard is dedicated to producing wines from native fruit and rootstock, following old-world techniques such as hand harvesting and fermenting in oak casks. The winery is housed in a chestnut-wood building that dates back to the 1700s. The vineyard was founded by Peter J. Kerensky, Sr., who was inspired by his father's home winemaking and his own love of cultivation. Kerensky planted his first grapes in 1953, and in 1979 was instrumental in passing Connecticut's Farm Winery Bill.

Although Peter Kerensky died in 1989, the Kerensky family continues to produce both grape and fruit wines. Daughter Meg Kerensky is the winemaker. She is pursuing a degree from the University of Connecticut in soil science and teaches courses in small-fruit management. The winery is owned and operated by the late Peter Kerensky's wife, Mary.

Except for the peaches, the Kerenskys grow all their own fruit. St. Hilary's Vineyard is best known for its fruit wines, and its Raspberry wine took a gold medal in Boston wine competitions in 1979-1981. The Kerenskys completed a new tasting room at the vineyard in June 1989.

Route 12
North Grosvenor Dale, CT 06225
203-935-5377

ESTABLISHED: 1979
FOUNDER: Peter J. Kerensky, Sr.
OWNER: Mary M. Kerensky
ACRES: 8
OUTPUT: 1,000 gallons
VISITING: Open daily 10-6, year round. Tastings daily, tours by appointment only.
DIRECTIONS: From Hartford or New Haven, take exit 98 off Route 395 and proceed on Route 12 north, going 1.08 miles past the junction of Route 12 and Route 131. From Worcester, Massachusetts, take Route 395 south to exit 100. Proceed on Wilsonville Road west to Route 12, turn left and go .25 mile to St. Hilary's.

WINES:
Golden Muscat
Captivator
Windham Red
Rosé
Van Buren
Blueberry
Peach
Raspberry

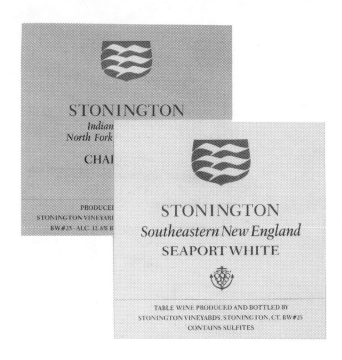

Co-owner Happy Smith calls Stonington 'a winery in progress.' Acreage is being expanded and buildings converted.

Stonington Vineyards

STONINGTON VINEYARDS WAS ESTABLISHED IN December 1986 when the Smiths purchased an existing vineyard and farm winery near the ocean in Stonington. The coastal climate provides a long, cool growing season and mild winters for the vineyard's Chardonnay, Pinot Noir, Riesling, and French-American hybrids—Seyval Blanc and Vidal. Winemaker Mike McAndrew ferments the grapes to a dry European style, aging them in French oak barrels. Stonington wines are sold throughout Connecticut in restaurants and wine shops.

The Smiths are full-time farmers and plan to keep Stonington Vineyards a small, high-quality operation. Until the expanded vineyards reach mature yields, and in order to increase the production of Chardonnay and Pinot Noir, the Smiths currently purchase grapes from a vineyard on Long Island's North Fork. Their goal is to produce 5,000-6,000 cases of predominantly estate-labeled wine.

Stonington Vineyards is 10 minutes from Mystic Seaport and the Mystic Aquarium, and the Smiths can recommend a variety of restaurants, bed and breakfasts, shopping, and other points of interest in the area.

Taugwonk Rd.
Stonington, CT
203-535-1222

ESTABLISHED: 1986
OWNERS: Nick and Happy Smith
ACRES: 10
OUTPUT: 4,500 cases
VISITING: Open daily from 11-5. Free tastings and tours. Call for tour schedule.
DIRECTIONS: From Interstate 95 north, take exit 91 (Stonington Borough). Turn left on Taugwonk Road, 2.4 miles. Vineyard on left. From Interstate 95 south, take exit 91. Turn right onto Taugwonk Road, 2.3 miles. Vineyard on left. From Route 2 south, turn right onto Route 184 at traffic circle. Go 2.3 miles, then left onto Taugwonk Road. Vineyard is 0.6 miles on the right.

WINES:
Vignoles
Estate Chardonnay
Estate Riesling
Estate Pinot Noir
✓ SEA PORT WHITE

Tasting diary

Wine _____

Winery _____ Year _____

Where purchased _____

Price _____ Date drunk _____

Occasion _____

Description _____

_____

_____

Wine _____

Winery _____ Year _____

Where purchased _____

Price _____ Date drunk _____

Occasion _____

Description _____

_____

_____

Wine _____

Winery _____ Year _____

Where purchased _____

Price _____ Date drunk _____

Occasion _____

Description _____

_____

_____

Wine _____

Winery _____ Year _____

Where purchased _____

Price _____ Date drunk _____

Occasion _____

Description _____

_____

_____

Wine _____

Winery _____ Year _____

Where purchased _____

Price _____ Date drunk _____

Occasion _____

Description _____

_____

_____

Wine _____

Winery _____ Year _____

Where purchased _____

Price _____ Date drunk _____

Occasion _____

Description _____

_____

_____

Wine _____

Winery _____ Year _____

Where purchased _____

Price _____ Date drunk _____

Occasion _____

Description _____

_____

_____

Wine _____

Winery _____ Year _____

Where purchased _____

Price _____ Date drunk _____

Occasion _____

Description _____

_____

_____

Wine _____

Winery _____ Year _____

Where purchased _____

Price _____ Date drunk _____

Occasion _____

Description _____

_____

_____

Wine _____

Winery _____ Year _____

Where purchased _____

Price _____ Date drunk _____

Occasion _____

Description _____

_____

_____

Wine _____

Winery _____ Year _____

Where purchased _____

Price _____ Date drunk _____

Occasion _____

Description _____

_____

_____

Wine _____

Winery _____ Year _____

Where purchased _____

Price _____ Date drunk _____

Occasion _____

Description _____

_____

_____

Wine _____

Winery _____ Year _____

Where purchased _____

Price _____ Date drunk _____

Occasion _____

Description _____

_____

_____

Wine _____

Winery _____ Year _____

Where purchased _____

Price _____ Date drunk _____

Occasion _____

Description _____

_____

_____

Wine _____

Winery _____ Year _____

Where purchased _____

Price _____ Date drunk _____

Occasion _____

Description _____

_____

_____

Wine _____

Winery _____ Year _____

Where purchased _____

Price _____ Date drunk _____

Occasion _____

Description _____

_____

_____

Wine _____

Winery _____ Year _____

Where purchased _____

Price _____ Date drunk _____

Occasion _____

Description _____

_____

_____

Wine _____

Winery _____ Year _____

Where purchased _____

Price _____ Date drunk _____

Occasion _____

Description _____

_____

_____

Wine _____

Winery _____ Year _____

Where purchased _____

Price _____ Date drunk _____

Occasion _____

Description _____

_____

_____

Wine _____

Winery _____ Year _____

Where purchased _____

Price _____ Date drunk _____

Occasion _____

Description _____

_____

_____

Wine _____

Winery _____ Year _____

Where purchased _____

Price _____ Date drunk _____

Occasion _____

Description _____

_____

_____

Wine _____

Winery _____ Year _____

Where purchased _____

Price _____ Date drunk _____

Occasion _____

Description _____

_____

_____

Wine _____

Winery _____ Year _____

Where purchased _____

Price _____ Date drunk _____

Occasion _____

Description _____

_____

_____

Wine _____

Winery _____ Year _____

Where purchased _____

Price _____ Date drunk _____

Occasion _____

Description _____

_____

_____

Wine _____

Winery _____ Year _____

Where purchased _____

Price _____ Date drunk _____

Occasion _____

Description _____

_____

_____

Wine _____

Winery _____ Year _____

Where purchased _____

Price _____ Date drunk _____

Occasion _____

Description _____

_____

_____

Wine _____

Winery _____ Year _____

Where purchased _____

Price _____ Date drunk _____

Occasion _____

Description _____

_____

_____

Wine _____

Winery _____ Year _____

Where purchased _____

Price _____ Date drunk _____

Occasion _____

Description _____

_____

_____

Wine _____

Winery _____ Year _____

Where purchased _____

Price _____ Date drunk _____

Occasion _____

Description _____

_____

_____

Wine _____

Winery _____ Year _____

Where purchased _____

Price _____ Date drunk _____

Occasion _____

Description _____

_____

_____

Wine _____

Winery _____ Year _____

Where purchased _____

Price _____ Date drunk _____

Occasion _____

Description _____

_____

_____

Wine _____

Winery _____ Year _____

Where purchased _____

Price _____ Date drunk _____

Occasion _____

Description _____

_____

_____

Wine _____

Winery _____ Year _____

Where purchased _____

Price _____ Date drunk _____

Occasion _____

Description _____

_____

_____

Wine _____

Winery _____ Year _____

Where purchased _____

Price _____ Date drunk _____

Occasion _____

Description _____

_____

_____

Wine _____

Winery _____ Year _____

Where purchased _____

Price _____ Date drunk _____

Occasion _____

Description _____

_____

_____

Wine _____

Winery _____ Year _____

Where purchased _____

Price _____ Date drunk _____

Occasion _____

Description _____

_____

_____

Wine _____

Winery _____ Year _____

Where purchased _____

Price _____ Date drunk _____

Occasion _____

Description _____

_____

_____

Wine _____

Winery _____ Year _____

Where purchased _____

Price _____ Date drunk _____

Occasion _____

Description _____

_____

_____

Wine _____

Winery _____ Year _____

Where purchased _____

Price _____ Date drunk _____

Occasion _____

Description _____

_____

_____

Wine _____

Winery _____ Year _____

Where purchased _____

Price _____ Date drunk _____

Occasion _____

Description _____

_____

_____

Wine _____

Winery _____ Year _____

Where purchased _____

Price _____ Date drunk _____

Occasion _____

Description _____

_____

_____

Wine _____

Winery _____ Year _____

Where purchased _____

Price _____ Date drunk _____

Occasion _____

Description _____

_____

_____

Wine _____

Winery _____ Year _____

Where purchased _____

Price _____ Date drunk _____

Occasion _____

Description _____

_____

_____

Wine _____

Winery _____ Year _____

Where purchased _____

Price _____ Date drunk _____

Occasion _____

Description _____

_____

_____

Wine _____

Winery _____ Year _____

Where purchased _____

Price _____ Date drunk _____

Occasion _____

Description _____

_____

_____

Wine _____

Winery _____ Year _____

Where purchased _____

Price _____ Date drunk _____

Occasion _____

Description _____

_____

_____

Wine _____

Winery _____ Year _____

Where purchased _____

Price _____ Date drunk _____

Occasion _____

Description _____

_____

_____

Wine _____

Winery _____ Year _____

Where purchased _____

Price _____ Date drunk _____

Occasion _____

Description _____

_____

_____

Wine _____

Winery _____ Year _____

Where purchased _____

Price _____ Date drunk _____

Occasion _____

Description _____

_____

_____

Wine _____

Winery _____ Year _____

Where purchased _____

Price _____ Date drunk _____

Occasion _____

Description _____

_____

_____

Wine _____

Winery _____ Year _____

Where purchased _____

Price _____ Date drunk _____

Occasion _____

Description _____

_____

_____

Wine _____

Winery _____ Year _____

Where purchased _____

Price _____ Date drunk _____

Occasion _____

Description _____

_____

_____

Wine _____

Winery _____ Year _____

Where purchased _____

Price _____ Date drunk _____

Occasion _____

Description _____

_____

_____

Wine _____

Winery _____ Year _____

Where purchased _____

Price _____ Date drunk _____

Occasion _____

Description _____

_____

_____

Wine _____

Winery _____ Year _____

Where purchased _____

Price _____ Date drunk _____

Occasion _____

Description _____

_____

_____

Wine _____

Winery _____ Year _____

Where purchased _____

Price _____ Date drunk _____

Occasion _____

Description _____

_____

_____

Wine _____

Winery _____ Year _____

Where purchased _____

Price _____ Date drunk _____

Occasion _____

Description _____

_____

_____

Wine _____

Winery _____ Year _____

Where purchased _____

Price _____ Date drunk _____

Occasion _____

Description _____

_____

_____

Wine _____

Winery _____ Year _____

Where purchased _____

Price _____ Date drunk _____

Occasion _____

Description _____

_____

_____

Wine _____

Winery _____ Year _____

Where purchased _____

Price _____ Date drunk _____

Occasion _____

Description _____

_____

_____

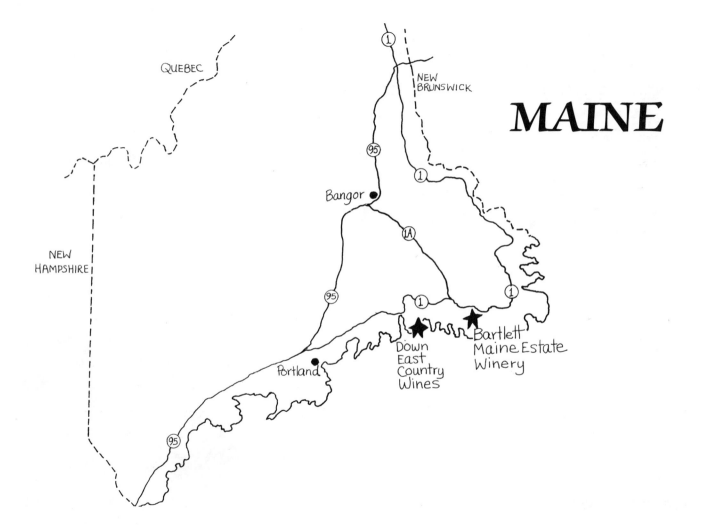

MAINE

QUEBEC

NEW BRUNSWICK

NEW HAMPSHIRE

Bangor

Portland

Down East Country Wines

Bartlett Maine Estate Winery

BRUT

Made in the Classic Methode Champenoi

CONTAINS SULFITES

PRODUCED AND BOTTLED BY BARTLETT MAINE ESTATE W
GOULDSBORO·MAINE·BW5·ALCOHOL 11% BY VOLUN

Bartlett
MAINE ESTATE WINERY

Raspberry Wine
s w e e t

Premium fruit wines of Maine

PRODUCED & BOTTLED BY
BARTLETT MAINE ESTATE WINERY·GOULDSBORO· ME
ALCOHOL 11.5% BY VOL·CONTAINS SULFITES

Bartlett
Maine Estate Winery

Apple Blush

a blend of 96% apple &
4% wild Maine blueberry wine

PRODUCED AND BOTTLED BY BARTLETT MAINE ESTATE WINERY
GOULDSBORO · ME · ALCOHOL 11.5% BY VOL·CONTAINS SULFITES

Bartlett Maine Estate Winery

ROBERT AND KATHE BARTLETT BOUGHT their land and designed and built their own house in Gouldsboro in 1975. Having a longstanding interest in wines, they planted grapes that summer, but they soon realized that the climate was too cold and the growing season too short for successful grape growing. The Bartletts abandoned their vineyard when Robert, a glass artist, was hired as a visiting artist at Ohio University. But their taste for wine and their love for Maine won out. In 1983 the Bartletts changed the state's wine legislation, became Maine's first winery, and began producing their first fruit wines.

Though fruit wines are traditionally sweet, the Bartletts also produce dry and semi-sweet wines, aging some wines in French oak casks specially made for them in California. The winery uses barrels of both French and American oak, as well as modern champagne and winemaking equipment.

Bartlett Maine Estate wines have done well in wine competitions. At the 1989 New England Wine Competition, their raspberry wine won the Best of Show award in the non-grape wine category. The dry blueberry took a gold medal, as did the raspberry, and, in addition, the winery won four silver medals and one bronze, making Bartlett Estate Winery the highest medal winner of all 95 grape and non-grape wines judged.

RR #1, Box 598
Gouldsboro, ME 04607
207-546-2408

ESTABLISHED: 1983
OWNERS: Robert and Kathe Bartlett
ACRES: none
OUTPUT: 16,000 gallons
VISITING: Open Tuesday through Saturday 10-5, Sunday 12-5, June to mid October. Closed on Mondays. Off season by appointment.
DIRECTIONS: Just off U.S. Route 1, 23 miles east of Ellsworth, in Gouldsboro. Maine State directional signs point the way to the winery.

WINES:
Apple
Apple Blush
Blueberry, dry, semi-dry, sweet
Blueberry Oak Reserve, dry
Blueberry Nouveau, dry
Coastal Red
Coastal White
Honey Mead, dry, semi-dry, sweet
Pear Oak Reserve, dry
Pear, dry, semi-dry
Sparkling Pear-Apple Brut
Raspberry
Strawberry

PRODUCED & BOTTLED BY DOWN EAST COUNTRY WINES, INC. BA...
CONTAINS SULFITES ALCOHOL 12% BY VOLUME

DOWN EAST COUNTRY WINES

SPICED
APPLE
WINE

*Apple Wine
With Spices Added*

DOWN EAST COUNTRY WINES

natural

WILD
BLUEBERRY
WINE

SEMI-SWEET

PRODUCED & BOTTLED BY DOWN EAST COUNTRY WINES, INC. BAR HARBOR, MAINE.
CONTAINS SULFITES ALCOHOL 11% BY VOLUME

Down East Country Wines

THOUGH SOME CONNOISSEURS MAY REFER to the Down East products as mere "farmhouse wines," owners Don Mead and Alison Wampler are proud of the country tradition that inspires their wines. The blueberry and apple wines of the Down East Country Winery come from old, locally developed recipes. The recipe for the acclaimed Medium Dry Wild Blueberry wine, for example, is 160 years old.

After being awarded two silver medals and a gold at the 1987 New England Wine Competition and a bronze at the InterVin international wine competition in Toronto, Canada, the Down East Country Winery was invited to present their wines to President Ronald Reagan in the Oval Office in September 1988. The Medium Dry Wild Blueberry wine was also tasted by Leningrad officials in 1989 when it was shipped on the S.S. *Maine* to the Soviet Union, and it has won the silver medal for two years running at the International Eastern Wine Competition.

Husband-and-wife team Mead and Wampler started the winery in 1987 in Pembroke, Maine, where it filled the first floor of their house. In 1987, the couple moved their growing business into a renovated blacksmith barn. Wampler, formerly a graphic designer in Boston, designs all the labels herself.

Route 3
Trenton, ME 04605
207-667-6965
ESTABLISHED: 1984
OWNERS: Don Mead and Alison Wampler
ACRES: none
OUTPUT: 39,000 bottles
VISITING: Monday through Saturday 9:30-6, Sunday 1-5, summer. Tuesday through Saturday 10-4, winter. Owners suggest that winter visitors call before visiting.
DIRECTIONS: 7 miles south of Ellsworth on Route 3.

WINES:
Blue Blush
Semi-Sweet Wild Blueberry
Medium Dry Wild Blueberry
Spiced Apple

Closed out of business

Tasting diary

Wine _____

Winery _____ Year _____

Where purchased _____

Price _____ Date drunk _____

Occasion _____

Description _____

_____

_____

Wine _____

Winery _____ Year _____

Where purchased _____

Price _____ Date drunk _____

Occasion _____

Description _____

_____

_____

Wine _____

Winery _____ Year _____

Where purchased _____

Price _____ Date drunk _____

Occasion _____

Description _____

_____

_____

Wine _____

Winery _____ Year _____

Where purchased _____

Price _____ Date drunk _____

Occasion _____

Description _____

_____

_____

Wine _____

Winery _____ Year _____

Where purchased _____

Price _____ Date drunk _____

Occasion _____

Description _____

_____

_____

Wine _____

Winery _____ Year _____

Where purchased _____

Price _____ Date drunk _____

Occasion _____

Description _____

_____

_____

Wine _____

Winery _____ Year _____

Where purchased _____

Price _____ Date drunk _____

Occasion _____

Description _____

_____

_____

Wine _____

Winery _____ Year _____

Where purchased _____

Price _____ Date drunk _____

Occasion _____

Description _____

_____

_____

Wine _____

Winery _____ Year _____

Where purchased _____

Price _____ Date drunk _____

Occasion _____

Description _____

_____

_____

Wine _____

Winery _____ Year _____

Where purchased _____

Price _____ Date drunk _____

Occasion _____

Description _____

_____

_____

Wine _____

Winery _____ Year _____

Where purchased _____

Price _____ Date drunk _____

Occasion _____

Description _____

_____

_____

Wine _____

Winery _____ Year _____

Where purchased _____

Price _____ Date drunk _____

Occasion _____

Description _____

_____

_____

Wine _____

Winery _____ Year _____

Where purchased _____

Price _____ Date drunk _____

Occasion _____

Description _____

_____

_____

Wine _____

Winery _____ Year _____

Where purchased _____

Price _____ Date drunk _____

Occasion _____

Description _____

_____

_____

Wine _____

Winery _____ Year _____

Where purchased _____

Price _____ Date drunk _____

Occasion _____

Description _____

_____

_____

Wine _____

Winery _____ Year _____

Where purchased _____

Price _____ Date drunk _____

Occasion _____

Description _____

_____

_____

Wine _____

Winery _____ Year _____

Where purchased _____

Price _____ Date drunk _____

Occasion _____

Description _____

_____

_____

Wine _____

Winery _____ Year _____

Where purchased _____

Price _____ Date drunk _____

Occasion _____

Description _____

_____

_____

Wine _____

Winery _____ Year _____

Where purchased _____

Price _____ Date drunk _____

Occasion _____

Description _____

_____

_____

Wine _____

Winery _____ Year _____

Where purchased _____

Price _____ Date drunk _____

Occasion _____

Description _____

_____

_____

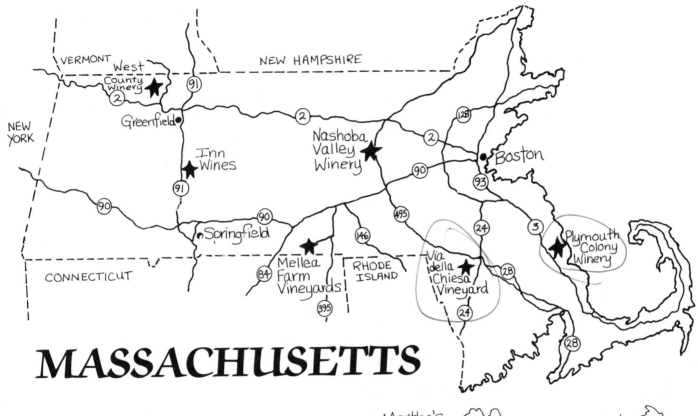

VERMONT

NEW HAMPSHIRE

West County Winery

NEW YORK

Greenfield

Inn Wines

NEW YORK

Springfield

CONNECTICUT

Nashoba Valley Winery

Boston

Mellea Farm Vineyards

RHODE ISLAND

Via della Chiesa Vineyard

Plymouth Colony Winery

2 91 2 128 90 93 495 24 3 28 24 146 84 395 28

MASSACHUSETTS

Martha's Vineyard

Chicama Vineyards

Nantucket

Nantucket Vineyard

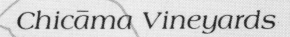

Chicāma Vineyards

Sea Mist
Sparkling Wine

BRUT

...t and Bottled by CHICAMA VINEYARDS
...bury, Martha's Vineyard, Massachusetts

...% by volume   Méthode Champenoise

CHICĀMA
VINEYARDS

American Table Wine

Gewurztraminer

Produced and Bottled by CHICAMA VINEYARDS
Stoney Hill Road, West Tisbury, MA 02575

Alcohol 12% by volume   BW-MA-1

Chicama Vineyards

MARTHA'S VINEYARD IS AN ISLAND in the Atlantic Ocean, five miles out from the Massachusetts coast. This maritime location affords long, warm autumns and fairly mild winters, ideal conditions for growing grapes. In addition to its climate, the island features a rich and varied soil—a result of the glacial terminal moraine. Because of these unique qualities, Martha's Vineyard has been determined a Viticultural Area by the U.S. Bureau of Alcohol, Tobacco, and Firearms.

George and Catherine Mathiesen have used the island's climate and soil to their advantage since 1971, when they founded the Chicama Vineyards (pronounced chi-kay-mah). The first bonded winery in Massachusetts, it is located in the small town of West Tisbury, the island's agricultural center. The Mathiesens specialize in growing vinifera varieties, including Chardonnay, Chenin Blanc, Cabernet Sauvignon, and Pinot Noir.

In addition to offering regular guided tours and tastings, Chicama has a retail winery shop stocked with wine vinegars, salad dressings, and chutneys, and a Christmas shop, open mid November through New Year's Eve.

Stoney Hill Road
West Tisbury, MA 02575
508-693-0309

ESTABLISHED: 1971
OWNERS: George and Catherine Mathiesen
ACRES: 18
OUTPUT: 15,000 gallons
VISITING: Tours and tastings Monday through Saturday 1-5, May. Monday through Saturday 11-5, Sunday 1-5, June through October. Friday and Saturday 1-4, shop and tastings only, January through April.
DIRECTIONS: Take the ferry from Woods Hole to Vineyard Haven on Martha's Vineyard. Leave Vineyard Haven on State Road toward West Tisbury and Gay Head. Turn left at Chicama Vineyards sign (2 1/2 miles from Vineyard Haven). Go 1 mile on gravel road.

WINES:

Chenin Blanc	Merlot
Chardonnay	Summer Island Red
White Zinfandel	Sea Mist
Satinet White	Cranberry-Apple
Sauvignon Blanc	Mayflower
Gewurztraminer	Cape Cod White
Zinfandel	
Cabernet Sauvignon	
Oceanus	

Though co-owner Dick Phaneuf says his sales are greatest in winter, visitors at that season miss seeing his farm garden in fruit. These are hops for his Honey Mead.

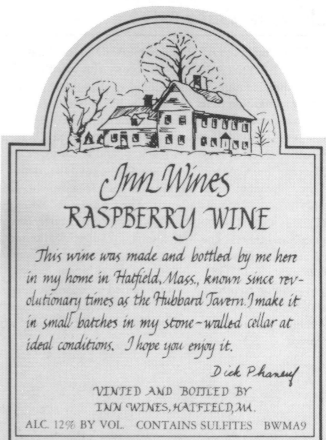

Inn Wines
RASPBERRY WINE

This wine was made and bottled by me here in my home in Hatfield, Mass., known since revolutionary times as the Hubbard Tavern. I make it in small batches in my stone-walled cellar at ideal conditions. I hope you enjoy it.

Dick Phaneuf

VINTED AND BOTTLED BY
INN WINES, HATFIELD, MA.

ALC. 12% BY VOL.   CONTAINS SULFITES   BWMA9

Inn Wines

A 20-YEAR-OLD HOBBY turned into a part-time business and what may be the smallest winery in New England when Richard Phaneuf and his wife Jan decided to sell his homemade wines. From the cellar of their home, a former inn that housed French troops during the Revolution, the owners of Inn Wines produce less than 1,000 gallons of wine a year.

Dick, a mechanical engineer, his wife, and their son Tom and daughter Deidre tend the four acres of fruit crops themselves and use no herbicides. Most of the fruit used in their wine is grown at the winery. Though the winery specialties are the rhubarb, blackberry, and raspberry wines, Inn Wines also sometimes offers elderberry, strawberry, gooseberry, apple, and pear wines. The Inn White and Inn Red are blends of grapes grown at the winery and in the area.

Located in the historic town of Hatfield, the Phaneuf home and winery was built in 1700. Along with its history as an Inn, the building also once served appropriately as the Hubbard Tavern.

4 Elm Street
Hatfield, MA
413-247-5175

ESTABLISHED: 1984
OWNERS: Richard and Janet Phaneuf
ACRES: 4
OUTPUT: less than 1,000 gallons
VISITING: Saturday and Sunday 11-6, May through December. Tastings during regular hours or by appointment. No tours given but grounds are open for exploration.
DIRECTIONS: 1.6 miles east of Interstate 91 at exit 21.

WINES:
Rhubarb
Blackberry
Raspberry
Mead (honey wine with hops)
Inn White
Inn Red
Peach

MELLEA VINEYARD

BROOKSIDE WHITE

A SOUTHEASTERN NEW ENGLAND

Dry White Wine

ALCOHOL 12% BY VOLUME

PRODUCED AND PACKED FOR MELLEA VINEYARD
BY THE HAMLET HILL WINES CO., POMFRET, CT

MELLEA VINEYARD
1988

COMPANION

A PREMIUM MASSACHUSETTS

Semi-Dry White Wine

ALCOHOL 12% BY VOLUME

PRODUCED AND PACKED FOR MELLEA VINEYARD
BY THE HAMLET HILL WINES CO., POMFRET, CT

Mellea Farm Vineyards

MELLEA VINEYARDS (PRONOUNCED MEL-LAY-AH) ARE positioned on a gently sloping hillside where grapes grow in maximum warmth and sunlight, summer and fall. The vines are hardy Seyval and Vidal, hybrids that can withstand the cold Massachusetts winter. Mellea's soil is a well-drained and sandy loam. The winery building is at the bottom of the hill, and wines produced there are made from Mellea's grapes as well as grapes from other New England vineyards.

Joseph—a semi-retired chemist—and Allie Campagnone started planting vines on their land in 1983, supplying grapes to commercial and home winemakers. In 1989 the Campagnones opened their own winery, asking their children to help run the business, and former home winemaker, Jed Roberts, to make their wine. The winery was named for Joseph Campagnone's mother.

Guests to Mellea Vineyards can tour the vineyard and wine cellar and browse in the gift corner. The vineyards are just 18 minutes from historic Sturbridge Village.

Old Southbridge Road
West Dudley, MA 01570
508-943-5166

ESTABLISHED: 1988
OWNER: Joseph A. Compagnone
OUTPUT: 1,000 cases
VISITING: Open Wednesday through Sunday 12-5, May through October. Saturday and Sunday 12-5, November and December. Tasting and tours are free; groups of 10 or more should reserve ahead.
DIRECTIONS: On Old Southbridge Road, off Massachusetts Route 131, north of Route 197, south of Route 20 and the Mass Turnpike.

WINES:
Harvest Gold
Brookside White
Companion
Cranberry-Apple

NANTUCKET VINEYARD

BARREL   AGED

NEW YORK
PINOT BLANC
1 9 8 9

NANTUCKET VINEYARD

NANTUCKET SLEIGHRIDE
WHITE TABLE WINE

NANTUCKET VINEYARD

WHITE
TABLE WINE

Nantucket Vineyard

SCENIC NANTUCKET VINEYARD, STARTED IN 1986 by Dean and
Melissa Long, is located near a beach, and is surrounded by 90 acres of
flower and vegetable gardens. The winery is small—its only distribution
is on Nantucket, an island 30 miles out from Cape Cod. Wine is
fermented in oak tanks in the Long's garage.

The Longs do all the work of winemaking and managing the vineyard
themselves. They grow some grapes on their seven-acre vineyard and
purchase others from vineyards in Long Island and Washington state.
Their wines are made from Pinot Blanc, Riesling, and Merlot grapes, with
some Cabernet and Pinot Noir used to make their blush wines. All of
their wines are grape wines.

3 Bartlett Farm Road
Nantucket, MA 02584
508-228-9235

ESTABLISHED: 1986
OWNERS: Dean and Melissa Long
ACRES: 7
OUTPUT: 30,000 bottles
VISITING: Open year round 10-5. Call ahead
in winter. No group tours.
DIRECTIONS: From the monument at the top
of Nantucket's Main Street, go 2.5 miles out
of town toward the island's South Shore on
Hummock Pond Road. Watch for the vine-
yard sign.

WINES:
Nantucket Sleighride
Pinot Blanc
Riesling
Savignon Blanc

Events such as the Apple Blossom Festival, shown here, are popular with visitors to Nashoba Valley Winery.

PLUM WINE

Maiden's Blush

A FRUIT WINE
MADE FROM 99% APPLES
AND 1% ELDERBERRIES

NASHOBA
V A L L E Y

PRODUCED AND BOTTLED BY NASHOBA VALLEY WINERY
BOLTON, MA BW-4   11% ALC/VOL   CONTAINS SULFITES

Nashoba Valley Winery

LOCATED JUST 45 MINUTES WEST of Boston, the Nashoba Valley Winery sits on a hill overlooking its 55-acre orchard. When owner Jack Partridge bought the site in 1984, the orchard was near extinction. Partridge now grows over 100 varieties of apples and other fruits used in Nashoba's fruit wines, including "antique" apples such as Winter Banana and Westfield-Seek-No-Further. Partridge and his staff have designed juice-extracting machinery, including a peach pitter-crusher for Nashoba's prizewinning After Dinner Peach.

Partridge, a former city planner, started selling wine from the basement of his home in Somerville, planting his one-fifth—acre backyard with apple and peach trees, blueberries, raspberries, and grapes. In 1980 Partridge moved the winery to West Concord, and four years later to its present quarters, building a new facility with that move. Nashoba Valley wines have won more than 50 medals in national and regional competitions.

Nashoba is an attractive spot for a picnic, and visitors can pick apples or take self-guided orchard tours. The winery is also the site of a variety of activities throughout the year, including the Apple Blossom Festival held in May, a Strawberryfest in June, and a September Harvest Festival.

100 Wattaquadoc Hill Road
Bolton, MA 01740
508-779-5521

ESTABLISHED: 1980
OWNER: Jack Partridge
ACRES: 55
OUTPUT: 7,000 cases
VISITING: Open daily 11-6, year round. Tastings and sales daily; tours Friday, Saturday, and Sunday.
DIRECTIONS: From Route 495 take Route 117 west (exit 27), 1 mile to Bolton Center. Turn left at the blinking light, .25 mile to winery.

WINES:
Baldwin Varietal Dry Apple
Maiden's Blush
Gravenstein Varietal Dry Apple
Cyser
Dry Pear
Cranberry-Apple
Orchard Run
Blueberry, semi-sweet, dry
Upland White
Plum
Winemaker's Reserve
After Dinner Peach
Strawberry
Upland Red
Raspberry

Visitors to Plymouth Colony Winery can walk through the bogs to see the ripening cranberries.

Plymouth Colony Winery

BUILT IN 1890, THE BUILDING now used for Plymouth Colony Winery was originally a cranberry screening house. In 1983 A. Charles Caranci, Jr., decided to take advantage of the healthful properties of cranberry juice by establishing a cranberry winery. All of the winery's cranberries are grown on the premises; in fact, the winery is in the middle of a 10.8-acre cranberry bog.

Some of Plymouth Colony's wines are made from a combination of cranberries and grapes, including their popular Bog Blush, which is 88% Seyval and Aurora grape and 12% cranberry. This wine has a distinct cranberry taste. Two of Plymouth's wines are strictly grape wines, Bog Blanc and Whale Watch White, while their award-winning Cranberry Grande is a 100% cranberry wine.

According to winemaker John LeBeck, making cranberry wine is difficult. Its high acidity requires a special yeast, something that was discovered only recently. LeBeck has spent 20 years in the wine business, including 3 years in the Finger Lakes region producing grape wines. He has seen the sales of Plymouth Colony's wines double in the past two years.

Though the town of Plymouth is busy, the winery's location is rural and scenic. Visitors drive down a lane surrounded by the bogs, and the cranberry plants are a striking red, changing to green during the growing season. The plants are in bloom in late April, and a cranberry harvest festival is held in early October. There is a picnic area on the premises, and tours and tastings are available.

Pinewood Road
Plymouth, MA 02360
508-747-3334

ESTABLISHED: 1983
OWNER: A. Charles Caranci, Jr.
ACRES: 10.8 of cranberries, 1 acre grapes (10 acres under contract elsewhere)
OUTPUT: 3,000 cases
VISITING: Open Monday through Saturday 10-5, Sunday 12-5, April 1 through January 1.
DIRECTIONS: From Route 3, exit 6, follow Route 44 west. Pinewood Road is exactly 3 miles on the left, opposite Clear Pond Motel. From the junction of Route 58 and Route 44, follow Route 44 east 4.8 miles to Pinewood Road on the right.

WINES:
Bog Blanc
Whale Watch White
Whale Watch Red
Bog Blush
Cranberry-Apple
Cranberry Grandé
Cranberry-Blueberry
Cranberry-Raspberry

Via della Chiesa's tasting area overlooks the vineyards, planted mostly in Cayuga White grapes.

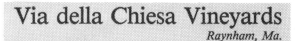

Via della Chiesa Vineyard

ROBERT DiCROCE SAYS IT WAS his Italian heritage that inspired him to start his own vineyard in Massachusetts. Via della Chiesa (or Church Street) Vineyards was conceived from DiCroce's pleasant memories of growing up in an Italian-Irish neighborhood in Brockton, Massachusetts, where Italians frequently made wine in their cellars for family and friends. Fifty years and a number of successful corporate ventures later, DiCroce, owner of a steel building construction company, has returned to a tradition passed down by his immigrant grandparents.

Tended by Hungarian winemaker Matyas Vogel, the vineyard and new winery are situated on the banks of the Taunton River, in the shadow of the the First Baptist Church. Via della Chiesa has 15 acres of Cayuga White grapes, a hybrid strain developed in Pennsylvania and New York to withstand cold and disease. Though the vineyard's output last year was only 6,000 gallons, DiCroce's output goal is 15,000-17,000 cases per year.

Via della Chiesa is minutes from the corporate headquarters of Ocean Spray and Cranberry World. The winery includes a tasting area with a glassed-in porch overlooking the vineyards and the surrounding countryside, and an adjoining balcony with a view of the wine cellars. Many hotels, motels, and restaurants are nearby.

513 Church Street
Raynham, MA 02767
508-822-7741
508-823-7777

ESTABLISHED: 1986
OWNER: Robert N. DiCroce
ACRES: 15
OUTPUT: 6,000 gallons
VISITING: Visitors are welcome May through October. Tours by appointment.
DIRECTIONS: Church Street is off Route 44 in Raynham, close to intersections of three major highways: Routes 495, 24, and 138.

WINES:
Cayuga-Muscat
Cranberry Delight
✓ CAYUGA - SUPREME

The sales and tasting room at West County is next to the Maloney's home, where they make hard cider and wines in their concrete basement.

West County Winery

WEST COUNTY WINERY—BONDED IN 1984—is the first New England winery to specialize in making hard ciders. Located in the township of Colrain, the winery uses apples—mainly Northern Spy and Baldwin—from the area's 11 hill-town orchards. In addition to ciders, the winery produces a peach wine in years of abundant peach harvest.

"Hard cider was the drink of the countryside for centuries," says Judith Maloney, who runs the winery with her husband Terry. "If you had apple trees—and up here, who didn't?—hard cider was part of the harvest. Apples were stored 'down cellar' in barrels; they were canned or dried; and they were pressed into jelly, vinegar, and cider—sweet at the pressing and hard after fermentation."

While living in California, the Maloneys were inspired by a Napa Valley friend who turned dairy land into vineyard. They gathered grapes, made wine, and talked with California winemakers. Coming to New England in 1972, the Maloneys saw the orchards of West County as raw material for a hard-cider revival. They made 350 gallons in the winery's first year, and they now produce 2,000 gallons. West County Winery's hard cider, light in alcohol (5.6% to 7%), is made with the same techniques used in producing fine wines.

The Maloneys hope to move their cider operation to a more accessible orchard by fall 1991. The winery will then be open to visitors throughout the year.

Box 123
Catamount Hill
Colrain, MA 01340
413-624-3481

ESTABLISHED: 1984
OWNERS: Judith and Terry Maloney
ACRES: 2
OUTPUT: 2,000 gallons
VISITING: Open Thursday through Sunday 11-5, September through November, and by appointment. Call ahead.
DIRECTIONS: Directions are available at Pine Hill Orchard on the Colrain-Greenfield Road, at Chandler's feed store, and at Stone's Sunoco station—all in Colrain.

WINES:
West County Cider
West County Dry Cider
West County Farm Cider
Orchard's Edge Apple-Raspberry Wine
West County Peach Wine

Tasting diary

Wine _____

Winery _____ Year _____

Where purchased _____

Price _____ Date drunk _____

Occasion _____

Description _____

_____

_____

Wine _____

Winery _____ Year _____

Where purchased _____

Price _____ Date drunk _____

Occasion _____

Description _____

_____

_____

Wine _____

Winery _____ Year _____

Where purchased _____

Price _____ Date drunk _____

Occasion _____

Description _____

_____

_____

Wine _____

Winery _____ Year _____

Where purchased _____

Price _____ Date drunk _____

Occasion _____

Description _____

_____

_____

Wine ———————————————

Winery ————————————— Year ————

Where purchased ————————————

Price ——————————— Date drunk ————

Occasion ——————————————

Description ——————————————

———————————————————

———————————————————

Wine ———————————————

Winery ————————————— Year ————

Where purchased ————————————

Price ——————————— Date drunk ————

Occasion ——————————————

Description ——————————————

———————————————————

———————————————————

Wine ———————————————

Winery ————————————— Year ————

Where purchased ————————————

Price ——————————— Date drunk ————

Occasion ——————————————

Description ——————————————

———————————————————

———————————————————

Wine ———————————————

Winery ————————————— Year ————

Where purchased ————————————

Price ——————————— Date drunk ————

Occasion ——————————————

Description ——————————————

———————————————————

———————————————————

Wine _____

Winery _____ Year _____

Where purchased _____

Price _____ Date drunk _____

Occasion _____

Description _____

_____

_____

Wine _____

Winery _____ Year _____

Where purchased _____

Price _____ Date drunk _____

Occasion _____

Description _____

_____

_____

Wine _____

Winery _____ Year _____

Where purchased _____

Price _____ Date drunk _____

Occasion _____

Description _____

_____

_____

Wine _____

Winery _____ Year _____

Where purchased _____

Price _____ Date drunk _____

Occasion _____

Description _____

_____

_____

Wine _____

Winery _____ Year _____

Where purchased _____

Price _____ Date drunk _____

Occasion _____

Description _____

_____

_____

Wine _____

Winery _____ Year _____

Where purchased _____

Price _____ Date drunk _____

Occasion _____

Description _____

_____

_____

Wine _____

Winery _____ Year _____

Where purchased _____

Price _____ Date drunk _____

Occasion _____

Description _____

_____

_____

Wine _____

Winery _____ Year _____

Where purchased _____

Price _____ Date drunk _____

Occasion _____

Description _____

_____

_____

Wine _____

Winery _____ Year _____

Where purchased _____

Price _____ Date drunk _____

Occasion _____

Description _____

_____

_____

Wine _____

Winery _____ Year _____

Where purchased _____

Price _____ Date drunk _____

Occasion _____

Description _____

_____

_____

Wine _____

Winery _____ Year _____

Where purchased _____

Price _____ Date drunk _____

Occasion _____

Description _____

_____

_____

Wine _____

Winery _____ Year _____

Where purchased _____

Price _____ Date drunk _____

Occasion _____

Description _____

_____

_____

Wine _____

Winery _____ Year _____

Where purchased _____

Price _____ Date drunk _____

Occasion _____

Description _____

_____

_____

Wine _____

Winery _____ Year _____

Where purchased _____

Price _____ Date drunk _____

Occasion _____

Description _____

_____

_____

Wine _____

Winery _____ Year _____

Where purchased _____

Price _____ Date drunk _____

Occasion _____

Description _____

_____

_____

Wine _____

Winery _____ Year _____

Where purchased _____

Price _____ Date drunk _____

Occasion _____

Description _____

_____

_____

Wine _____

Winery _____ Year _____

Where purchased _____

Price _____ Date drunk _____

Occasion _____

Description _____

_____

_____

Wine _____

Winery _____ Year _____

Where purchased _____

Price _____ Date drunk _____

Occasion _____

Description _____

_____

_____

Wine _____

Winery _____ Year _____

Where purchased _____

Price _____ Date drunk _____

Occasion _____

Description _____

_____

_____

Wine _____

Winery _____ Year _____

Where purchased _____

Price _____ Date drunk _____

Occasion _____

Description _____

_____

_____

Wine _____

Winery _____ Year _____

Where purchased _____

Price _____ Date drunk _____

Occasion _____

Description _____

_____

_____

Wine _____

Winery _____ Year _____

Where purchased _____

Price _____ Date drunk _____

Occasion _____

Description _____

_____

_____

Wine _____

Winery _____ Year _____

Where purchased _____

Price _____ Date drunk _____

Occasion _____

Description _____

_____

_____

Wine _____

Winery _____ Year _____

Where purchased _____

Price _____ Date drunk _____

Occasion _____

Description _____

_____

_____

Wine _____

Winery _____ Year _____

Where purchased _____

Price _____ Date drunk _____

Occasion _____

Description _____

_____

_____

Wine _____

Winery _____ Year _____

Where purchased _____

Price _____ Date drunk _____

Occasion _____

Description _____

_____

_____

Wine _____

Winery _____ Year _____

Where purchased _____

Price _____ Date drunk _____

Occasion _____

Description _____

_____

_____

Wine _____

Winery _____ Year _____

Where purchased _____

Price _____ Date drunk _____

Occasion _____

Description _____

_____

_____

Wine _____

Winery _____ Year _____

Where purchased _____

Price _____ Date drunk _____

Occasion _____

Description _____

_____

_____

Wine _____

Winery _____ Year _____

Where purchased _____

Price _____ Date drunk _____

Occasion _____

Description _____

_____

_____

Wine _____

Winery _____ Year _____

Where purchased _____

Price _____ Date drunk _____

Occasion _____

Description _____

_____

_____

Wine _____

Winery _____ Year _____

Where purchased _____

Price _____ Date drunk _____

Occasion _____

Description _____

_____

_____

Wine _____

Winery _____ Year _____

Where purchased _____

Price _____ Date drunk _____

Occasion _____

Description _____

_____

_____

Wine _____

Winery _____ Year _____

Where purchased _____

Price _____ Date drunk _____

Occasion _____

Description _____

_____

_____

Wine _____

Winery _____ Year _____

Where purchased _____

Price _____ Date drunk _____

Occasion _____

Description _____

_____

_____

Wine _____

Winery _____ Year _____

Where purchased _____

Price _____ Date drunk _____

Occasion _____

Description _____

_____

_____

Wine _____

Winery _____ Year _____

Where purchased _____

Price _____ Date drunk _____

Occasion _____

Description _____

_____

Wine _____

Winery _____ Year _____

Where purchased _____

Price _____ Date drunk _____

Occasion _____

Description _____

_____

Wine _____

Winery _____ Year _____

Where purchased _____

Price _____ Date drunk _____

Occasion _____

Description _____

_____

Wine _____

Winery _____ Year _____

Where purchased _____

Price _____ Date drunk _____

Occasion _____

Description _____

_____

Wine _____

Winery _____ Year _____

Where purchased _____

Price _____ Date drunk _____

Occasion _____

Description _____

_____

_____

Wine _____

Winery _____ Year _____

Where purchased _____

Price _____ Date drunk _____

Occasion _____

Description _____

_____

_____

Wine _____

Winery _____ Year _____

Where purchased _____

Price _____ Date drunk _____

Occasion _____

Description _____

_____

_____

Wine _____

Winery _____ Year _____

Where purchased _____

Price _____ Date drunk _____

Occasion _____

Description _____

_____

_____

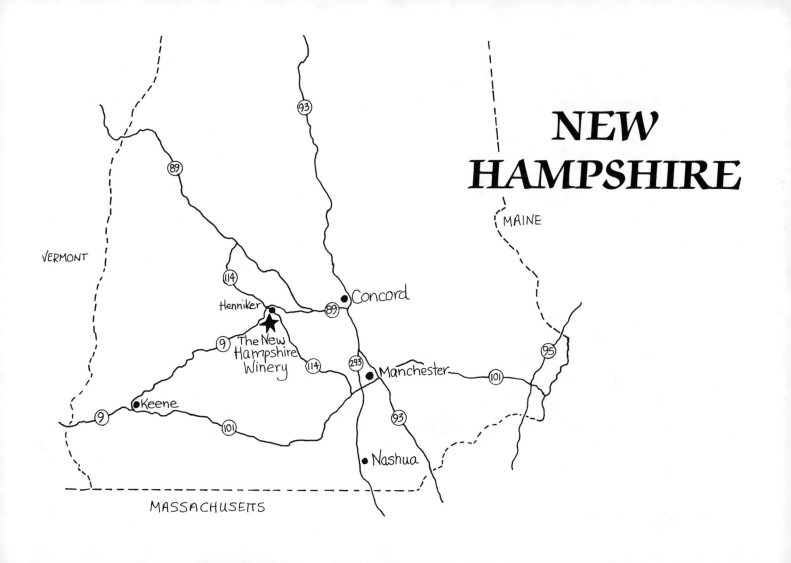

Seyval and other grapes bought from local vineyards are used at the New Hampshire Winery.

Passings   Nancy Glassman

The New Hampshire Winery

LIBERTY HILL

SAUVIGNON BLANC

VINTED AND BOTTLED BY THE NEW HAMPSHIRE WINERY
HENNIKER, NEW HAMPSHIRE
ALCOHOL 12.5% BY VOLUME   NHBW NO. 3

The New Hampshire Winery

THE NEW HAMPSHIRE WINERY, STARTED in 1964 by John Canepa, was the first commercial winery in New England. Canepa, a chemist and fruit grower who retired to New Hampshire, turned the winery over to the Howard family in 1985, and in December 1989 the winery moved to its present location in Henniker. Since then it has been run by Bill Damour, who is also the winemaker.

Bill Damour doesn't grow grapes at his site in Henniker, but purchases grapes and juices from local vineyards. Varieties used for his grape wines include Marechal Foch, Seyval Blanc, De Chaunac, and others. His planned output for 1990 is 13,500 gallons.

The setting for the winery is pastoral and scenic. It's surrounded by pastureland, and it rests at the foot of Pat's Peak ski area. The winery building is of post-and-beam construction, and houses modern, stainless steel winemaking equipment and French oak barrels. Visitors to the New Hampshire Winery can view the bottling-room and wine-cellar procedures through glass walls. As tour and tasting hours may change seasonally, visitors are asked to call ahead.

38 Flanders Road
Henniker, NH 03242.
603-428-9463

ESTABLISHED: 1964
OWNERS: New England Spirits
OUTPUT: 5,000 gallons, 13,500 planned for 1990
VISITING: Tastings and tours available daily 10-5, year round. Call ahead.
DIRECTIONS: From Route 89, take exit 5 and drive 10 miles west on Route 202 to Route 114. The winery is 2.5 miles south of the village of Henniker, at the foot of Pat's Peak.

WINES:
Cabernet
Chardonnay
Sauvignon Blanc
Dry Colombard
White Zinfandel
Marechal Foch
Spiced Apple
Raspberry Dessert

Tasting diary

Wine ——————————————————————

Winery ———————————————— Year ——————

Where purchased ————————————————————

Price ———————————————— Date drunk ——————

Occasion ——————————————————————

Description ——————————————————————

——————————————————————————

——————————————————————————

Wine ——————————————————————

Winery ———————————————— Year ——————

Where purchased ————————————————————

Price ———————————————— Date drunk ——————

Occasion ——————————————————————

Description ——————————————————————

——————————————————————————

——————————————————————————

Wine ——————————————————————

Winery ———————————————— Year ——————

Where purchased ————————————————————

Price ———————————————— Date drunk ——————

Occasion ——————————————————————

Description ——————————————————————

——————————————————————————

——————————————————————————

Wine ——————————————————————

Winery ———————————————— Year ——————

Where purchased ————————————————————

Price ———————————————— Date drunk ——————

Occasion ——————————————————————

Description ——————————————————————

——————————————————————————

——————————————————————————

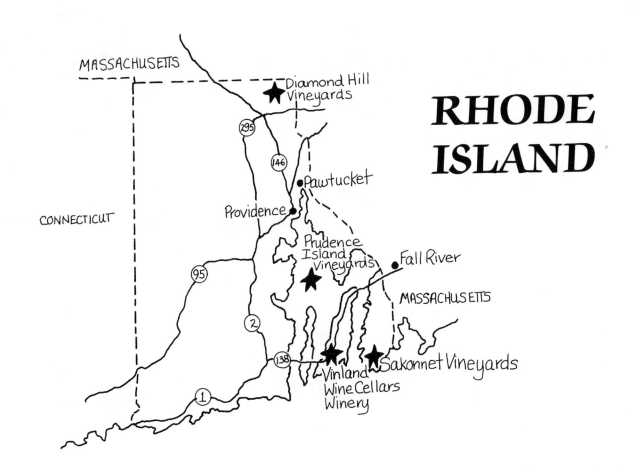

MASSACHUSETTS

Diamond Hill
Vineyards

RHODE
ISLAND

CONNECTICUT

295

146

Pawtucket

Providence

95

Prudence
Island
Vineyards

Fall River

MASSACHUSETTS

2

138

Vinland
Wine Cellars
Winery

Sakonnet Vineyards

1

Diamond Hill's tasting and sales rooms are on the ground floor of this 200-year-old farmhouse.

Diamond Hill Vineyards

DIAMOND HILL VINEYARDS, NAMED AFTER the nearby state park, is the only one of the four wineries in Rhode Island that produces wine from fruit other than grapes. It is also one of a few in New England that makes wine from both grapes and other fruits.

The winery's first commercial release was its 1983 Pinot Noir in 1986, but, because of the long time it took to prepare the grape varieties, owners Peter and Claire Berntson decided to branch out to peach, apple, and berry wines. Though the Berntsons buy the berries and other fruits from farms in Maine, Rhode Island, and Connecticut, the Pinot Noir grapes are all cultivated at Diamond Hill Vineyard.

Diamond Hill grape and fruit wines have been recognized as outstanding in the region. Their peach wine was awarded a gold medal in 1987 at the New England Wine Competition, and the Pinot Noir 1986 received a silver medal at the same competition in 1989.

Situated in the historic Blackstone River Valley, the post-and-beam building which houses the winery's modern equipment was built by Peter and Claire Berntson. The vineyard residence, a 200-year-old farm house with spacious grounds, is frequently the site of group picnics catered by the Berntson family. The Berntson's gift shop features customized wine labels and New England and Rhode Island foods.

3145 Diamond Hill Road
Cumberland, RI
401-333-2751

ESTABLISHED: founded 1976, bonded 1979
OWNERS: Peter and Claire Berntson
ACRES: 4.5
OUTPUT: 1,500 cases
VISITING: Open all year. Weekdays 12-5, Saturday 10-5, Sunday 12-5, closed Tuesday. Tours on Sundays May through October or by appointment. Tasting every day when open.
DIRECTIONS: From Route 295 take exit 11. Proceed north on Route 114 (Diamond Hill Road). Go 2 miles to stone gates and sign on the right.

WINES:
Golden Apple
Pommes Blanc
Pommes Blush
Peach
Blueberry
Strawberry
Pinot Noir
Pinot Noir Blanc
Cranberry-Apple
Spiced Apple

Prudence Island Vineyards

In Narragansett Bay

Rhode Island

Gamay Beaujolais

1983

Produced and Bottled by Prudence Island Vineyards

Prudence Island, Rhode Island 02872

Alcohol 11% by Volume   *B.W.R.I. 2*

Prudence Island Vineyards

WILLIAM BACON AND HIS WIFE came to Prudence Island after their children were grown and educated, making Mrs. Bacon's six-generation family farm their permanent home. They cleared the land for grapes in 1973, wanting to take up the family tradition of farming that was abandoned with the hurricane of 1938 in which Mrs. Bacon's father lost his barn. The Bacons initially made their wine in an old milk house, but in 1978 they built an underground winery. Son Nathanael Bacon is the vineyard manager, and William, winemaker.

Though Prudence Island Vineyards is no longer producing wine other than for the Bacon family's home use—1988 was the last vintage—the Bacons still have a stock of Chardonnay and Pinot Noir for sale, and the vineyard is open for tours and tastings. William Bacon advises that visitors call ahead, as a trip to Prudence Island is dependent upon the ferry schedule. The ferry ride from Bristol takes about half an hour. Prudence Island contains 1,400 acres of state-park land and large deer population, and in clear weather visitors can see across Narragansett Bay to as far as Providence on Rhode Island's mainland.

Sunset Hill Farm
Prudence Island, RI 02872
401-683-2452

ESTABLISHED: 1973
OWNERS: the Bacon family
ACRES: 12
VISITING: Call ahead anytime.
DIRECTIONS: Walk up the hill from the Prudence ferry landing. Take a right at the top of the hill. Proceed between vineyards to the house.

WINES:
Chardonnay
Pinot Noir

At Sakonnet, a self-guided tour of the vineyards and grounds affords views of the Sakonnet River. The house in the vineyards can be rented for business meetings and other functions.

Sakonnet Vineyards

IN SPITE OF ITS QUIET location at the end of a winding dirt road, Sakonnet Vineyards houses the largest winery in New England. Earl and Susan Samson bought the vineyard in 1987 from founders Jim and Lolly Mitchell, who had planted its first vines. Earl, a former venture capitalist, and Susan, a former actress, added new equipment, upgrading the electrical and septic systems, and planting more grapes.

Sakonnet produces 11 wines, and since the vineyard's inception, has won many awards. Its Chardonnay was featured in *Gourmet* magazine, the Pinot Noir won a silver medal in the American Wine Competition, and the Vidal Blanc has repeatedly taken Best of Class award in the Eastern International Wine Competition. This last wine was served to Prince Charles in Boston in 1987, and Sakonnet wines were served at President George Bush's inauguration.

Sakonnet produces about 80% of its wines from French-American hybrids, but four of its wines are varietals: Chardonnay, Gewurztraminer, Vidal Blanc, and Pinot Noir. Sakonnet's winemaker believes that Vidal Blanc is the most successful of these and thinks Sakonnet's reputation may rest on that wine. The Samsons like to promote their wines as companions to food, and they have offered cooking classes at the winery with regionally well-known guest chefs.

162 West Main Road (Route 77)
Little Compton, RI 02837
401-635-8486

ESTABLISHED: 1975
FOUNDERS: Jim and Lolly Mitchell
OWNERS: Earl and Susan Samson
ACRES: 40
OUTPUT: 22,000 cases
VISITING: Open Monday through Saturday 11-5, Sundays 12-5, November through April. Daily 10-6, May through October. Closed Easter, Thanksgiving, Christmas, and New Year's Day. Tours are available on the hour, May through October on Wednesday, Saturday, and Sunday. Group tours by appointment.
DIRECTIONS: Go south on Route 77, through traffic light at Tiverton Four Corners. Sakonnet is 3 miles further on the left.

WINES:

Chardonnay	Compass Rose
Gewurztraminer	Rhode Island Red
Vidal Blanc	Nouvelle
Pinot Noir	Nouveau
America's Cup White	
Spinnaker White	
Eye of the Storm Blush	

VINLAND

Newport Hospitality White

A NEWPORT COUNTY SEMI-SWEET TABLE WINE
GROWN, PRODUCED & BOTTLED BY
VINLAND WINE CELLARS, MIDDLETOWN, R.I.

HOPELANDS 1988 VINEYARDS

VINLAND

Viking Red

A NEWPORT COUNTY DRY TABLE WINE
GROWN, PRODUCED AND BOTTLED BY
VINLAND WINE CELLARS, MIDDLETOWN, R.I.

HOPELANDS 1988 VINEYARDS

American and French oak barrels are used for aging at Vinland, a cooperative winery on Aquidneck Island near Newport.

Vinland Wine Cellars Winery

ALTHOUGH IT TAKES ITS NAME from Leif Ericsson's ancient Norse settlement thought possibly to have been in Rhode Island, Vinland Wine Cellars Winery is one of the newest and most modern wineries in New England. Founded in 1988 by retired naval Captain Richard Alexander and his wife Hope, the winery is located on Aquidneck Island, the island in Narragansett Bay after which Rhode Island was named.

Vinland is a cooperative winery, with many grape growers contributing fruit and sharing the company's profits. One of these vineyards is Hopelands, owned and planted by the Alexanders on their 22-acre estate along the Sakonnet River in Middletown. Hopelands Vineyards was first planted in 1977 as a way for the Alexanders to preserve the farmland estate inherited from Mrs. Alexander's mother. It is the source of four of the nine wines that Vinland produces—Newport Hospitality White, Viking Red, Island Blush, and Gemini. Both Island Blush and Newport Hospitality White received bronze medals in the 1989 International Eastern Wine Competition.

Vinland also produces Seyval Blanc and Vidal Blanc, both made from grapes from the Finger Lakes area of New York, and a Riesling and a Rochambeau from grapes grown on Long Island. Vinland's first Chardonnay, also made from Long Island grapes, was released in October 1989.

909 East Main Road
East Gate Center
Middletown, RI 02840
401-848-5161
800-345-1559

ESTABLISHED: winery 1988, tasting room 1989
OWNERS: Captain Richard and Hope Alexander
ACRES: 22
OUTPUT: 24,000 gallons
VISITING: Open Monday through Saturday 10-5, Sundays 12-5. Closed Christmas Day, Thanksgiving Day, and New Year's Day.
DIRECTIONS: The winery is part of the Eastgate Center in Middletown on East Main Road (Route 138), nearly opposite the Newport State Airport. Look for the Eastgate Center with winery sign and flags across from Chaves Garden Center.

WINES:
Newport Hospitality White
Vidal Blanc
Riesling
Seyval Blanc
Island Blush
Viking Red
Chardonnay
Gemini
Rochambeau

Tasting diary

Wine _____

Winery _____ Year _____

Where purchased _____

Price _____ Date drunk _____

Occasion _____

Description _____

_____

_____

Wine _____

Winery _____ Year _____

Where purchased _____

Price _____ Date drunk _____

Occasion _____

Description _____

_____

_____

Wine _____

Winery _____ Year _____

Where purchased _____

Price _____ Date drunk _____

Occasion _____

Description _____

_____

_____

Wine _____

Winery _____ Year _____

Where purchased _____

Price _____ Date drunk _____

Occasion _____

Description _____

_____

_____

Wine _____

Winery _____ Year _____

Where purchased _____

Price _____ Date drunk _____

Occasion _____

Description _____

_____

_____

Wine _____

Winery _____ Year _____

Where purchased _____

Price _____ Date drunk _____

Occasion _____

Description _____

_____

_____

Wine _____

Winery _____ Year _____

Where purchased _____

Price _____ Date drunk _____

Occasion _____

Description _____

_____

_____

Wine _____

Winery _____ Year _____

Where purchased _____

Price _____ Date drunk _____

Occasion _____

Description _____

_____

_____

Wine _____

Winery _____ Year _____

Where purchased _____

Price _____ Date drunk _____

Occasion _____

Description _____

_____

_____

Wine _____

Winery _____ Year _____

Where purchased _____

Price _____ Date drunk _____

Occasion _____

Description _____

_____

_____

Wine _____

Winery _____ Year _____

Where purchased _____

Price _____ Date drunk _____

Occasion _____

Description _____

_____

_____

Wine _____

Winery _____ Year _____

Where purchased _____

Price _____ Date drunk _____

Occasion _____

Description _____

_____

_____

Wine _____

Winery _____ Year _____

Where purchased _____

Price _____ Date drunk _____

Occasion _____

Description _____

_____

_____

Wine _____

Winery _____ Year _____

Where purchased _____

Price _____ Date drunk _____

Occasion _____

Description _____

_____

_____

Wine _____

Winery _____ Year _____

Where purchased _____

Price _____ Date drunk _____

Occasion _____

Description _____

_____

_____

Wine _____

Winery _____ Year _____

Where purchased _____

Price _____ Date drunk _____

Occasion _____

Description _____

_____

_____

Wine _____

Winery _____ Year _____

Where purchased _____

Price _____ Date drunk _____

Occasion _____

Description _____

_____

_____

Wine _____

Winery _____ Year _____

Where purchased _____

Price _____ Date drunk _____

Occasion _____

Description _____

_____

_____

Wine _____

Winery _____ Year _____

Where purchased _____

Price _____ Date drunk _____

Occasion _____

Description _____

_____

_____

Wine _____

Winery _____ Year _____

Where purchased _____

Price _____ Date drunk _____

Occasion _____

Description _____

_____

_____

Wine _____

Winery _____ Year _____

Where purchased _____

Price _____ Date drunk _____

Occasion _____

Description _____

_____

_____

Wine _____

Winery _____ Year _____

Where purchased _____

Price _____ Date drunk _____

Occasion _____

Description _____

_____

Wine _____

Winery _____ Year _____

Where purchased _____

Price _____ Date drunk _____

Occasion _____

Description _____

_____

_____

Wine _____

Winery _____ Year _____

Where purchased _____

Price _____ Date drunk _____

Occasion _____

Description _____

_____

Wine _____

Winery _____ Year _____

Where purchased _____

Price _____ Date drunk _____

Occasion _____

Description _____

_____

_____

Wine _____

Winery _____ Year _____

Where purchased _____

Price _____ Date drunk _____

Occasion _____

Description _____

_____

_____

Wine _____

Winery _____ Year _____

Where purchased _____

Price _____ Date drunk _____

Occasion _____

Description _____

_____

_____

Wine _____

Winery _____ Year _____

Where purchased _____

Price _____ Date drunk _____

Occasion _____

Description _____

_____

_____

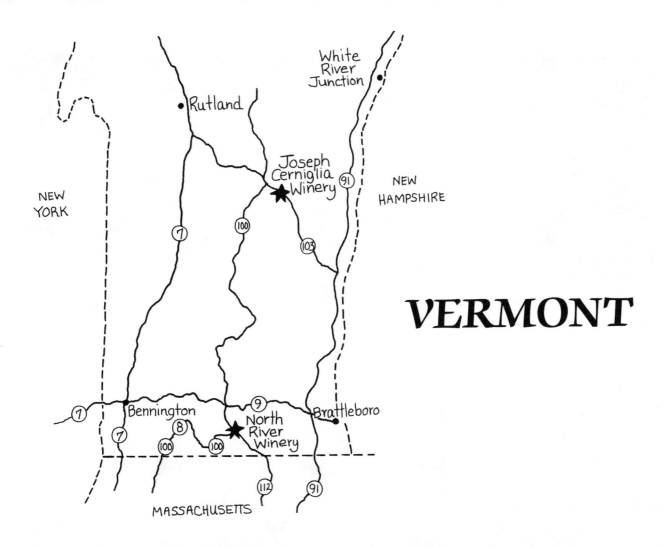

Dedicated to our friend
Vincent Valk

Vincent

Raspberry
DESSERT WINE
100% RASPBERRY

Contains sulfites

Joseph Cerniglia
Cavendish, VT U
1 • 800 • 654 • 6382   1 •

VERMONT

OLD
FASHIONED

RD CIDER

12% ALC./VOL.

Bottled by Joseph Cerniglia Winery, Inc.
ndish, Vermont USA BWVT3

Joseph Cerniglia
Winery

NORTHERN SPY

Limited Reserve

Apple Wine

Produced and Bottled by Joseph Cerniglia Winery, Inc.,
Cavendish, Vermont USA   BWVT3   11% ALC./VOL.

Joseph Cerniglia Winery

JOSEPH CERNIGLIA WINERY, ONE OF the largest in New England, specializes in varietal apple wines. These 100% single-juice wines range from dry to sweet, and all varieties go with a large range of foods.

A former stockbroker from New York City, Joseph Cerniglia purchased the 200-acre Double Four Apple Orchard in 1978. However, after a vacation to California where he became enchanted with the vineyards there, and after strong winds blew down his apple crop, leaving it to rot on the ground, Cerniglia decided to try making his own apple wine. He and his wife Elfreda were joined by Gregory Failing, a winemaker with 18 years of experience, who left his job at a large grape winery to come to Vermont.

The winery, which has been visited by an estimated 30,000 tourists, is on the shore of the Black River. It produces apple, pear, and raspberry wine, as well as hard cider, wassail, and wine coolers. All the apples for the varietal wines except the Granny Smiths are grown by Cerniglia in his own orchards. Cerniglia wines, now distributed in 14 states, have won awards and notice throughout the Northeast as well as at the 1989 74th National Orange Show where the Perry and Northern Spy wines were given gold medals. The Cerniglia winery is dedicated to Joseph's immigrant grandfather Guiseppe Cerniglia, whose picture appears on the wine labels.

Winery Road, Route 103
Proctorsville, VT 05153
802-226-7575

ESTABLISHED: 1986
OWNER: Joseph Cerniglia
ACRES: 45 acres of orchards
OUTPUT: 54,000 gallons
VISITING: Open daily 10-5, year round. Free tours and tastings 10-4:15 daily.
DIRECTIONS: On Route 103, just south of Ludlow, VT.

WINES:
Granny Smith
Empire
McIntosh
Golden Delicious
Red Delicious
Northern Spy
Macoun
Perry (pear wine)
Raspberry
Vermont Hard Cider
Nouveau Sap Water

METCALFE'S HARD CIDER

from Vermont

ENGLISH STYLE CIDER

Produced and Bottled by North River Winery
Jacksonville, VT · BW-VT-1 · Alcohol 9% by Volume

CONTAINS SULFITES

NORTH RIVER WINERY

**VERMONT
BLUSH**

DRY

96% APPLES / 4% RASPBERRIES

VERMONT FRUIT TABLE WINE

Produced and Bottled by North River Winery
Jacksonville, Vermont · BW-VT-1
Alcohol 11% by Volume

North River Winery

ED METCALFE, A FORMER SCHOOLTEACHER and hot-air balloonist, started North River Winery in 1985. At that time it was the only winery in Vermont. Before coming to Vermont, Metcalfe managed a liquor store in Rhode Island, taught a wine appreciation course at a community college, worked at Sakonnet Vineyards—a Rhode Island winery—and tried his hand at amateur winemaking. Metcalfe's North River operations were initially housed in a single room in his restored 1850s barn in Jacksonville. This included his sales area, bottling equipment, and two 800-gallon fermentation tanks. Since then, the winery has expanded into other parts of the barn, and Metcalfe has nine fermentation tanks.

North River Winery produces nine fruit wines made of raspberries, blueberries, cranberries, and a variety of apples. They range in taste from Vermont Blush—a dry dinner wine—to Blueberry-Apple—a sweet wine that serves as an aperitif or dessert wine. Metcalfe buys all of his apples from nearby orchards, and uses relatively unknown apple varieties such as Winesap, Jonathan, and Rhode Island Greening. Metcalfe also makes a hard cider, lower in alcohol than wine.

Jacksonville is a small village with a general store, community church, and white clapboard houses. The winery is just south of town on the banks of the North River, a river lined with sugar maples.

River Road, Route 112
Jacksonville, VT 05342
802-368-7557

ESTABLISHED: 1985
OWNERS: Edward C. Metcalfe and Linda Cardone
ACRES: 2 of orchard
OUTPUT: 12,000 gallons
VISITING: Open daily 10-5, May through December. Friday, Saturday, and Sunday 11-5, January through April. Tours run continuously during visiting hours.
DIRECTIONS: On Route 112, 6 miles south of Wilmington.

WINES:
Vermont Blush
Green Mountain Apple
Woodland Red
Cranberry-Apple
Raspberry Apple
Vermont Harvest
Blueberry-Apple
Metcalfe's Hard Cider
Northern Spy

Tasting diary

Wine _____

Winery _____ Year _____

Where purchased _____

Price _____ Date drunk _____

Occasion _____

Description _____

_____

_____

Wine _____

Winery _____ Year _____

Where purchased _____

Price _____ Date drunk _____

Occasion _____

Description _____

_____

_____

Wine _____

Winery _____ Year _____

Where purchased _____

Price _____ Date drunk _____

Occasion _____

Description _____

_____

_____

Wine _____

Winery _____ Year _____

Where purchased _____

Price _____ Date drunk _____

Occasion _____

Description _____

_____

_____

Wine _____

Winery _____ Year _____

Where purchased _____

Price _____ Date drunk _____

Occasion _____

Description _____

_____

_____

Wine _____

Winery _____ Year _____

Where purchased _____

Price _____ Date drunk _____

Occasion _____

Description _____

_____

_____

Wine _____

Winery _____ Year _____

Where purchased _____

Price _____ Date drunk _____

Occasion _____

Description _____

_____

_____

Wine _____

Winery _____ Year _____

Where purchased _____

Price _____ Date drunk _____

Occasion _____

Description _____

_____

_____

Wine _____

Winery _____ Year _____

Where purchased _____

Price _____ Date drunk _____

Occasion _____

Description _____

_____

_____

Wine _____

Winery _____ Year _____

Where purchased _____

Price _____ Date drunk _____

Occasion _____

Description _____

_____

_____

Wine _____

Winery _____ Year _____

Where purchased _____

Price _____ Date drunk _____

Occasion _____

Description _____

_____

_____

Wine _____

Winery _____ Year _____

Where purchased _____

Price _____ Date drunk _____

Occasion _____

Description _____

_____

_____

New England's Wine Grapes

HYBRID VARIETIES

Aurora—white French-American hybrid, produces soft, fragrant wine, often used as a base for champagne

Baco Noir—popular red French-American hybrid, can produce a slightly herbaceous wine

Cascade—red French-American hybrid used for rosé and red table wine

Cayuga White—white hybrid grape developed in U.S. by the New York Geneva Experiment Station

Chancellor—red French-American hybrid, produces a dark red wine

Concord—native American hybrid, produces grapey-tasting, usually sweet wine; also used as base for most grape juices, jellies, and candies

Leon Millot—red French-American hybrid, early ripening, similar to Marechal Foch

Marechal Foch—red French-American hybrid, produces a hearty, deep-colored wine

Seyval Blanc—white French-American hybrid suited to cool climates, produces a fruity wine

Vidal Blanc—popular white French-American hybrid, produces a fruity wine

Vignoles (Ravat)—white French-American hybrid, produces a dry wine

VINIFERA VARIETIES

Cabernet Franc—red vinifera grape often used in blends

Cabernet Sauvignon—red vinifera grape, the principal red grape of Bordeaux, France

Chardonnay—white vinifera grape, produces a fruity, dry white wine

Chenin Blanc—white vinifera grape, produces a slightly sweet wine

Gewurztraminer—white vinifera grape, produces delicate to spicy wines

Muscadet—white vinifera grape, produces a dry white wine

Pinot Meunier—red vinifera grape

Pinot Noir—red vinifera grape, the principal red grape of Burgundy, France

Riesling—white wine produced from any vinifera grape variety with the name Riesling, slightly sweet to sweet

Zinfandel—red vinifera grape

Wine Vocabulary

aperitif—generic term for before-dinner wine or other drink to stimulate appetite

aroma—the part of the smell of a wine that comes from the grape itself, not the smell developed in the bottle; may predominate in young wine, whereas bouquet predominates in mature wine

Beaujolais Nouveau—young, fruity red wine made for drinking within a few months of its vintage

blush—a rosy or pinkish wine usually made from red grapes by brief maceration of skins, where the color is

bottle aging—the gradual maturing and mellowing of wines

Botrytis cinerea—a mold or fungus that attacks grapes, causing a concentration of sugar and acid, and thus flavor; beneficial when grapes are ripe and when the goal is rich wine

bouquet—the pleasant smell of wine; the odor created by the wine's own development in the bottle

chablis—generic name for white table wine; a wine from Chablis, France, made from Chardonnay, very dry

champagne—sparkling wine made from Pinot Noir, Pinot Meunier, and Chardonnay; in the U.S., generic term for sparkling wine

champagne method (méthode champenoise)—the process for making sparkling wine in which the wine undergoes a second fermentation in the bottle, trapping carbon dioxide bubbles

chaptalization—addition of sugar during fermentation to increase the alcohol content of a wine when grapes do not contain optimal sugar concentration

complex—said of wine with many tastes and smells, indicative of well-developed, fine wine

crush—the breaking of the grape skins that begins the winemaking process

degorgement—removal by hand of sediment in sparkling wines, part of the champagne method

dry—not sweet

enology—see oenology

farm winery—a winery that makes wine from grapes that its own vineyards have produced; estate winery

fermentation—biochemical process by which the sugar in juice is converted into alcohol and carbon dioxide by the action of yeast enzymes

foxy—the tangy flavor associated with wines made from native American grapes

fruit—the flavors and aromas of the source fruit

fruit wine—wine made from fruits other than grapes

green—said of the acidic taste of wine made from immature grapes, or taste of immature wine

harden off—the process plants go through to get ready for winter temperatures

hybrid—cross of grapes of two different species, for example, native American grapes with viniferas, e.g., French-American hybrids

mead—honey wine

nose—a broad term for the smell of a wine

oenology—the science of making wine

Phylloxera vastatrix—a plant louse (aphid) that attacks vinifera vine roots and destroyed nearly all vinifera vines in the late 19th century

port—generic name for sweet, fortified wine, usually red

rootstock—a root and its associated growth buds, used as stock in plant propagation and for grafting vinifera to protect against Phylloxera

rosé—light, pinkish wine made for early consumption

sparkling wine—wine with carbon dioxide bubbles

still wine—non-sparkling wine

tannin—astringent-tasting compound, especially in young red wines

varietal—a wine named after the predominant grape variety in its composition

vineyard—plantation of grapevines for production of wine

vinification—process of making wine

vinous—pertaining to wine; applied to the taste of wine

vintage—the year's grape harvest

viticultural area—a federally recognized region where wine grapes are grown, smaller than a state; if the region's name is used on a label, 85% of the wine must be from grapes grown there

viticulture—the science of cultivating the vine and producing grapes

Vitus vinifera—species of old-world grape vine used in the production of fine wines

winery—an establishment for producing wine

New England Wine Organizations

IF YOU ARE INTERESTED IN learning more about New England wineries and vineyards, here are some regional wine organizations you can contact.

New England Wine Council, c/o Earl Samson, Sakonnet Vineyards, 162 West Main Road, Little Compton, RI 02837, 401-635-8486.

Southeastern New England Grape Growers Association, c/o Joetta Kirk, Sakonnet Vineyard, 162 West Main Road, Little Compton, RI 02818, 401-635-8486.

The Connecticut Vineyard and Winery Association, c/o Barbara DiGrazia, DiGrazia Vineyards and Winery, 131 Tower Road, Brookfield Center, CT 06805, 203-775-1616.

The *New England Wine Gazette*, edited by Nancy Knowles Parker, is published quarterly. You can subscribe by sending $10 for one year to the Recorder Publishing Co., 17-19 Morristown Road, Bernardsville, NJ 07924. The phone number of *New England Wine Gazette's* editorial office is 401-847-3268.